WHODUNIT

Investigating Industrial Accidents

Marc-André Poisson

Foreword by Stephen Blank

Whodunit

Library and Archives Canada Cataloguing in Publication

Title:	Whodunit / Investigating Industrial Accidents / The Search for The Impossible Truth
Description:	Essay on industrial accidents investigation
	Includes bibliographical references and index.
Identifiers:	ISBN 978-2-9819505-0-5 (softcover)
	ISBN 978-2-9819505-1-2 (PDF)
	ISBN 978-2-9819505-2-9 (EPUB)
Subjects LCSH:	Industrial accidents - Canada - Investigation - Industrial accidents in literature - Cognitive psychology - Failure mode and effects analysis - Truth - Post-truth - Deception

Published in Canada by Sphérik

Production Credits

Cover and graphic elements:	Rumeur promo-design
Proofreading:	Judy Yelon
Editor:	Jim McRae
Contributing Editor:	Jacques Kéroack

Printed in Canada

Dépôt légal – Bibliothèque et Archives nationales du Québec, 2021.

Table of Contents

Foreword

"Captain in Mauritius Oil Spill Disaster Is Arrested." This is the headline of an article from the *New York Times* of August 18, 2020. Three days earlier, a Japanese-owned Panama-flagged bulk carrier ran aground near Mauritius and broke in half, spilling at least 1,000 tons of oil into the Indian Ocean and endangering world-renowned coral reefs and lagoons. Sunil Kumar Nandeshwar, the captain, was arrested and charged with endangering the safe navigation of a vessel, an offence under Mauritian maritime laws. The Times article stated that *"Local news media reported that a preliminary examination by the police showed the crew was having a party on the night the ship ran off course."* (Dahir, 2020)

Maritime accidents are not unusual. Thousands occur each year, of which 50 or so can be classified as "disasters." Nor is the outcome of this investigation unusual. The initial judgment was quick and focused on one person. It answers our need to find a culprit - to respond to the whodunit demand.

This is where Captain Marc-André Poisson's book begins, with the standard procedure of many accident investigations. Investigators are under pressure to move quickly and identify the causes and those responsible. The theme of Poisson's book is that this is not good enough, that this approach does not tell us enough about what happened or, most importantly, lay the foundation for improving safety.

In a career of 37 years in the safety and security field, Poisson concluded that the pressure for a Whodunit answer was understandable. But the answer was not enough to build a meaningful picture of how and why these accidents occurred. "Linear causation" - an analysis that focuses events as they occur in an orderly system, and pinpoints a single individual or a single event - is insufficient. *If you are investigating an industrial accident, you are not searching for a culprit.*

The culprit - the cause of the accident - is rarely a single person, rarely a single error or misjudgment. Almost always, many factors interact in a series of interrelated developments that result in the accident. Too often, investigators get off on the wrong foot. *"They start with pre-established beliefs. Then, they look for evidence to support them. This is also how we normally react when we want to find out causes and contributing factors for an occurrence at home, at work, or in our community. We want to know who is at fault."* Instead, Poisson says, we need to look at the entire safety system - or absence of a safety system.

Poisson wants investigators to study the human factors that lead to the occurrence or disaster. He says they must be able to comprehend the societal paradigm at the source of occupational accidents - the social, economic, and political environment in which the accident occurred, which shaped the events leading to the accident. These factors cannot be viewed as individual, isolated events, but must be seen instead as deeply interconnected, interactive elements of a wider system or "culture."

"We can stop more 737 MAXes from inducing a dive, but we may not be able to describe the system that created the aircraft. To prevent more disasters from happening, we may need to identify underlying causes and contributing factors that lead to the in-service operation of new aircraft. We should try to understand the systems that create machines, plants, and high-tech engineering projects."

Poisson's experience surely qualifies him for this task. His career touches all of the marks. He is the former Director of Marine Investigations at the Transportation Safety Board of Canada and immediate past Chair of the Marine Accident Investigators'

International Forum. In 2017, the International Maritime Organization (IMO) appointed Poisson as an IMO Maritime Goodwill Ambassador, a nomination that prompted him to start the Canadian Marine Industry Foundation in 2019. He holds a master's degree in marine policy from the University of Wales, Cardiff. He has many publications to his credit and is a recipient of the Canadian Coast Guard's highest award, the exemplary service medal.

He does not lack hands-on practice: Poisson commanded a Search and Rescue vessel, going out in storms to rescue people. From 2000 to 2008, he was directly involved in every major disaster or catastrophic event in Canada. As senior policy advisor or director in the federal government, he was able to see the impacts and failures of government and industry. He participated in developing policy, memoranda to cabinet, and coordinating national responses, an eye-opener, he has said, on the complexities of preparing, preventing, responding, and recovering from disasters, natural and human made.

Poisson felt that his experience and education enabled him to understand that investigators were not going far enough in some of their investigations. *"We were excellent in identifying the immediate causes and contributing factors that lead to the disaster, but we were not very proficient in studying the systems that create disasters. I wanted to research what we were doing right and identify areas where we were failing. Someone needed to investigate the way we investigate failure."*

The book has much to say about improving investigation techniques, about improving teamwork and multidisciplinary collaboration. But this is not just an upgraded manual for investigators. Poisson digs deeply into the intellectual frameworks that lie behind and support investigation. Accident causation models used by investigators around the world are limited. *"We clearly need to use new theories, given that the traditional objectivist models and theories have not helped us shift systemic behaviours."* Much of the volume is an assessment of the various theories to develop systemic investigation models.

This takes us into deeper waters, about how we acquire knowledge and determine, in Poisson's terms, *what is real*. He guides us through a library of investigatory theories and then dives into their philosophical and sociological sources. He cites Freud, Feyerabend, Flyvbjerg and Gödel to name but a few. He states that the book *"can be said to be a postmodern approach to investigating failure as it confronts the ideological, social, and historical structures that shape and constrain the production of an investigation report."*

The going can be tough, but his aim is clear: To understand what caused an accident and the risk factors that exist in the workplace, the theoretical models must examine the impacts of the external and internal environments while understanding the interactions of a work structure with its effects and its results. *"We need to develop a workable model that allows researchers and practitioners to dig deep down to uncover the next level of underlying factors that will permit us to understand how the evolving systems are affected and work... We also need to encourage debates on the knowledge that is produced and how investigation bodies construct their findings."*

He looks intently at the relationship of theory and practice. This is the buckle between the two dimensions of Poisson's study.

I believe Poisson asked me to write this Foreword because of my long interest in transportation. That's true, but I find more resonance with my work as an historian. The historian's craft is similar to that of the accident investigator - to reconstruct a past event or series of events. We both seek to make sense out of a basket of data points. We seek to understand how these data points relate to each other - and try to tease out patterns of cause and effect.

The historian's dilemma is that we know how the story works out. That knowledge shapes how we tell the story: We naturally focus on the factors and developments that inevitably lead to this end. But people involved at the time do not know how it will end. They may not see what we later view as a critical development. Voices which we later understand as instrumental to the outcome may at the time be lost in the crowd. The danger is that our stories become too neat, leading inevitably to the conclusion, and missing the vital elements of uncertainty, doubt, and confusion at the time.

This is why the search for the culprit in an accident investigation can blind us to the wider factors that shaped the accident.

Historians, too, suffer as we view data through our own societal, economic, and personal filters. We struggle to release ourselves from the intellectual constraints that interpret what we see. "Where we sit is where we stand": The old line about political beliefs can be the same for historians, and for accident investigators, too. Histories can reveal as much about authors and their time as the subject of the works.

And we also struggle with finding a balance in the dialectic between personal and environmental causal forces. Some historians have positioned themselves at the far ends of this range. Historians have focused on individual biography as the key to events - some even seeking to delve into the psyche of a long dead subject. Others have seen individuals and events as phenomena of underlying environmental forces - think of Marx.

For generations, historians have sought to march to the tune of *wie es eigentlich gewesen* - tell it how it really was. The same as accident investigators. But this might be a fruitless task. The great historian, Edward Hallett Carr tried to set us straight: *"The historian is necessarily selective,"* he wrote. *"The belief in a hard core of historical facts existing objectively and independently of the historian is a preposterous fallacy, but one which it is very hard to eradicate. It used to be said that the facts speak for themselves. This is, of course, untrue. The facts speak only when the historian calls on them: it is he who decides to which facts to give the floor, and in what order of context."* (Carr, 1986)

This is what Poisson wants to help us understand - how the accident investigator "calls" on the data, what factors shape how this is done and how it can be done better.

In our work, Marc-André and I share many interests and face many similar problems. But in the end, a very powerful difference between us exists.

There's a clear bottom line in his work: *The only purpose of investigation work should be to improve the lives of our fellow humans... Investigators need to always keep in mind that their work has to improve safety. Their quest for data is not about accumulating knowledge purely for the purpose of producing it. It is about producing practical wisdom pursuant to research and investigation.*

That's why this book is important. It is a demand for better investigatory techniques, a model that will focus primarily on identifying a way to build safer environments.

Stephen Blank
Roosevelt Island, New York
September 10, 2020

Preface

The inspiration to write this essay comes from our propensity to doubt. For me, it began in the fifth grade when I learned the concept of infinity. My teacher asked the class to walk towards the wall by taking a step that was only half as big as the prior one. We had to pause and think. We made the first steps quite easily, laughing as it became more and more difficult the closer we got to the wall. How could we subtract a half a millimeter? Half of nothing! I was dumbstruck. I just could not figure out how to split the infinitesimal figures that I was trying to imagine.

Everyone was flabbergasted when the teacher stopped us and said, "Theoretically, you should never reach the wall. One-half of a half is always a half of something. It goes to infinity." Wow! The concept is mind-boggling when you stop and think about never reaching a wall you can actually touch with your hand. Immediately I began to question what I had learned: Was he telling me the truth?

I share concepts I began learning in the early 1980s when I spent a few semesters taking mandatory philosophy classes. My mind raced at the thought that, as humankind evolved, knowledge that was thought to be true was sometimes wrong. I started to suspect that all that I had learned and was about to learn could most likely be erroneous.

During my undergrad studies, I watched the BBC film series *The Ascent of Man*, based on a personal appreciation of human history written and presented by Prof. Jacob Bronowski. Bronowski explained the knowledge of things and the laws that govern them as the natural result of the quest by humans for their survival, their cultural adaptation, and their intelligence: the unique gift that distinguishes us from other animals. He recounted the facts and described the evolution of scientific models and contemporary technologies. It encouraged me to deepen my knowledge of the opposition between the real and the ideal, between empiricism and dogmatism. I was and remain fascinated by the fact that today's truth is tomorrow's falsehood. Our search for the truth never ends and never will.

After completing Coast Guard College and sailing with the fleet for a few years, I took a few courses in physics at university. Upon returning to sea, I spent part of my leisure time reading about quantum physics, mainly the works of Max Planck, Albert Einstein, and Werner Heisenberg, three of the most celebrated scientists of their time. Heisenberg won the 1932 Nobel Prize for creating quantum mechanics that describes nature at the smallest size scale. He is also known for the uncertainty principle, which states that we cannot determine the exact position and momentum of a particle simultaneously. If we determine one of them exactly, we cannot determine the other at the same time. The uncertainty principle is a solid result that says - my words - we can never know everything about anything.

The book is my perspective of work, research and examples of failure that I have assembled. It is a reflection on how we perceive and conceive reality and communicate our findings as professionals in the field of accident investigations.

I no longer conduct investigations. I am now a member of the Transportation Appeal Tribunal of Canada, appointed by Her Excellency the Governor in Council, on the recommendation of the Minister of Transport. By agreement with the policy of the Government of Canada, I do not divulge privileged or confidential information, nor is it necessary for the purpose of this book. I only use data that is in the public domain. The ideas in this essay are the sole responsibility of the author.

I hope that you will see my work for what it is meant to be: a new perspective on a field that improves our lives. Based on my education and experience, I question what is true in investigation reports. Who is at fault? What broke down in the system? Whodunit?

Marc-André Poisson
Ottawa
September 12, 2020

Introduction

This book covers a lot of ground. Not only does it present theories and knowledge that illustrate the complexities of identifying the parties involved in the cause of an accident, it also introduces the science behind communicating the truth, a very current topic in this age of fake news and false claims. Simultaneously, and fully aware of the irony, I take certain liberties with the truth myself, but only to avoid pointing blame towards any individual. For example, when discussing a disaster, I will improvise names and also introduce tidbits of information to create a more compelling story. However, at no point do I alter the facts contained within the official accounts of reports, which led authorities to draw their conclusions that I enumerate in order to introduce the science and techniques behind a very complex task.

The book presents a different perspective, a different lens through which to view the field and also the science of accident investigation and reporting. I try to uncover the flaws in investigation work while keeping in mind the areas of investigations that need improvement. While I provide key information used by professionals, scientists, and technicians, I do not claim this book to be the "gospel." I do hope, nevertheless, to enlighten you as to how I conducted my work to uncover my version of the truth.

Finally, I do not leave the reader hanging. I provide solutions to a way forward in a world that has become unintelligible. I conclude this voyage into the work and minds of investigators with a path to help us understand failure and the truth that can improve safety. The key may lie with the idea that we can make some sense out of the first level of chaos that exists when we create new work environments and new transportation systems.

HOW TO READ THIS BOOK

The book is divided into five chapters aimed at answering the main question *Whodunit?* Each chapter contains an essay-type first section, which tells the dramatic story of an actual accident, including key facts related to the event. The second section comprises theories, science, and practices that an investigator would use to uncover or explain the causes and contributing factors related to the accident. The third section is *Closing Arguments*, summing up the chapter.

Throughout each chapter, additional features help bolster the information, including accounts of other accidents and an *Investigator's Maze* comprising critical questions an investigator could be asking about the main accident that is introduced. Each chapter starts with a list of the theories or concepts being examined under the title *Looking for Clues*. The overarching goal is a dual-purpose book, one that can serve as an interesting read for a layperson with a passion for accident investigations, or a hard-working tool for any professional studying the discipline.

THE CONTENT

Chapter 1 explores how we make errors in everyday life - big and small - and why it is always easy to find someone else to blame for them. The chapter will help readers realize that investigation theory is not very hard to comprehend. We use it in our everyday lives and it is actually intuitive for us.

Chapter II is a bit technical, but a must-read if you want to learn how rudimentary investigative work is done. It covers the standard scientific theories used by most investigators, and, intriguingly, a forgotten one. Readers will discover that imperfect theories, including those that fall prey to subjectivity, are the backbone of systemic investigative work, and how there is no such thing as a deterministic theory, a topic explored in detail in Chapter IV.

Chapter III covers the social perspective of faults. It shows you that we see things differently according to our birthplace, our gender, our cultural background, and our position in a work environment. It also shows you the steps to take if you want to launch your own investigation.

Chapter IV is largely based on doctoral papers I authored. I aim to demonstrate that there is no such thing as the truth, neither in science nor in safety investigations. You will learn that finding out whodunit can be an impossible task. The truth may take different forms and can even evolve. Investigators, like scientists, acquire knowledge. Their goal is to find the truth that will improve safety.

Finally, Chapter V provides various perspectives on communicating the truth, including all the versions I encountered over my 35-year career as an emergency responder, emergency manager, investigator, trainer, and spokesperson in the international maritime field. You will learn how we communicate, or should communicate, whodunit.

Let's begin our investigation!

I

The Main Culprit
Mea culpa

› *Truth comes in different forms*
› *The science of error*
› *Slips, lapses, and mistakes*
› *Poorly adapted plans*
› *Human performance*

In 2010, the Canadian sail training vessel *Concordia* was 900 kilometres off the coast of Brazil making her way north in winds of 30 knots (56 kilometres per hour). John, Mary, and Paul were on deck while the rest of the crew were below decks, along with the 48 high school students on board who were getting into the seats of the small classrooms that they had crammed into for the day's history and mathematics lessons. Water splashed onto the portholes from the breaking waves, and while seasickness was no longer a critical issue - most had earned their "sea legs" a few days back - not everyone had shaken its effects; it was difficult to focus in the floating classroom. From time to time, large waves interrupted the class by crashing on the hull, temporarily drowning out the hum of the vessel as it made its way in the southern Atlantic Ocean.

Billy was at the helm. He had joined the vessel at age 24. With very little background and training, he was at the start of what he believed to be an enriching career. Second officer of the *Concordia* was the perfect job, he thought: sailing the world, eating well, and getting paid. He enjoyed the company of keen crew members, enthusiastic academic staff, and creative adolescents. What more could he ask for? Certainly not what Poseidon was about to offer: a sea god's humour in the form of conditions that would mark his life forever.

The 57-metre vessel had encountered small squalls since leaving Recife. On 16 February, Ryan, the master, had received the Brazilian Navy Marine Meteorological Service weather forecasts through satellite communications. They forewarned of wind backing from the southeast/east, increasing to Beaufort (empirical measure of wind speed) force 7 or 8 with gusts up to 75 kilometres an hour. The edges of wave crests would break into spindrift and foam would blow in well-marked streaks along the direction of the wind. Ryan informed the ship's complement of the approaching weather.

On the morning of 17 February, the master shortened sail. The sail plan included an inner jib, fore staysail, upper and lower topsails, main staysail, main, and mizzen sails; only the mizzens were reefed. The plan was conservative, neither pushing for speed, nor leaning on the side of temerity. That's what the captain and the second officer thought.

Ryan instructed Billy to keep a comfortable heel (ship inclination angle) during class lesson time, and to avoid squalls. Both discussed the actions to take if they needed to reduce sail. Ryan went below to rest. Billy was in charge and enjoying every minute. He was maintaining course, and both speed and heel were per captain's instructions. About an hour later, a few crew members on deck observed three squalls on the horizon, which Billy tracked visually and also on radar. It became clear that one of the squalls would intersect the vessel's course. It was different from the other squalls encountered over the previous days, and although it seemed to contain more rain, there were no visible whitecaps on the sea. For the moment, it was steady as she goes.

The wind soon began to pick up, causing the *Concordia* to heel a bit more. The vessel's windows and doors on the windward side were all open. The air was entering the vessel freely, with the sound of the gusts echoing throughout the passageways. John was filming a video and Mary took a picture at exactly the same moment that the *Concordia* reached the maximum heeling angle just as the squall hit. Nobody could guess the impact.

Wind can hit without notice and often hides its power. The wind is a hypocrite. The vessel heeled further to port until the bridge wing was about to go under water. Billy was pressing the helm's joystick until the rudder angle indicator read hard over. He also managed to grab hold of Mary, who was in danger of falling overboard through a gap in the rail and had yelled for help. He brought her to the reception area behind the wheelhouse on the starboard side. He then called Ryan. Water was now entering through the port wheelhouse door, and the anemometer showed an apparent wind speed of 30 knots. The vessel struggled to right itself, made all the harder with the excessive sea water on deck, but was eventually knocked down, succumbed by the conditions, and on its beam ends. The crew, teaching staff, and students evacuated into life rafts where they spent the next two days bobbing on the ocean before help arrived. The *Concordia* would disappear to the bottom of the Atlantic Ocean, a total loss.

The National Oceanic and Atmospheric Administration (NOAA) studied satellite and global forecast system data from February 17, the day the *Concordia* went down. The data showed that three key weather conditions had converged. NOAA concluded that this caused a severe microburst, or downburst, that likely hit the ship with downward winds in excess of 120 kilometres per hour. "I'm very certain that this was a severe downburst to be able to capsize a ship like that," said the meteorologist from his office in Camp Springs, MD. "I was able to identify satellite signatures or features that corresponded directly to a microburst occurrence." The features included a notch of dry air feeding a thunderstorm. This provided the energy for very strong winds.

This theory fit well with what the crew suspected. The intense winds blasted so quickly that it had to be a microburst that struck the ship. Before NOAA's input, nobody had data to support these suspicions. The vessel owner mentioned, "It confirms for me the narrative that was initially reported back to our office by our captains and crew (…). We've always believed that it was an extreme weather event and suspect that the investigation may well bear that out." (Canadian Press, 2010)

Upon my arrival as Head of Marine Investigations at Canada's Transportation Safety Board (TSB), the first international challenge I faced was the submission, by the Barbados authorities, of a report about the Canadian-owned sailing training vessel *Concordia*, flagged under their jurisdiction. The report submitted to the International Maritime Organization (IMO) was unequivocal: a microburst was the culprit. End of story. Case closed. Both a professional mariner - the Barbados investigator - and a U.S. meteorologist were on the same page as the crew. A rare weather phenomenon, an intense blast of air, hit and capsized the *Concordia* moments before it sank off the Brazilian coast.

My predecessor at the TSB had decided to launch a parallel investigation. I therefore arrived in the midst of the Canadian investigation, which was still ongoing as Barbados published their report that made perfect sense to me, as I had witnessed the impacts of unexplained - freak - weather events at sea and lived through many storms as a professional mariner. I was also, because of my different studies and experiences, set on the path of doubting the assertion that one owns the truth. I was also fortunate to count on a great investigation team.

The Canadian investigation found that the wind speeds experienced by the vessel at the time of the knockdown were most likely in the range of 25 to 50 knots (46 to 93 kilometres per hour). "While there was probably a vertical component to the wind, there is no evidence that a microburst occurred at the time of the knockdown." The crew operated the vessel in a way that did not allow it to "... react to changing weather conditions appropriately and maintain the stability of the vessel." (TSB M10F0003)

Many disputed our findings, including that we claimed that the wind and wave conditions were most likely no different from what the vessel had encountered many times before. We calculated the stability conditions. The sail plan was set in a condition that left the vessel vulnerable to a squall of less than 30 knots. These are normal conditions. We had John's video and Mary's photographic evidence taken moments before the knockdown that were used to build a model that would lead to the development of irrefutable calculations. The Barbados authorities, the master, and the U.S. expert were most likely wrong. There may have been a microburst, but the vessel did not need a microburst to push it on its side. It was vulnerable to even normal wind conditions at the time of capsizing. You can read the public report for yourself and examine the findings.

TRUTH CAN TAKE DIFFERENT FORMS

I chose this story to open Chapter I of this book in order to show that we can draw different and very probable conclusions about the same disaster. The truth can take different forms. Investigators produce knowledge in the form of findings as to causes, contributing factors, and risks. They choose from, amongst an infinite number of ideas, what they decide to study and publish, aiming to provide the best information to help avoid another accident. They focus on the most probable causes, often limiting the number of contributing factors and risks that are present in the system. The report that you read, or the conclusions that you hear an investigator state in a press conference, is the version of the most probable story that will have the greatest impact on safety. One of my overall goals with this book is to show you how investigators create this story.

The number of safety issues we can uncover in each investigation is endless. We need to stop at a certain point and choose what we are going to focus on. In the *Concordia* investigation, we decided not to belabour the reason why there were so many entry points for seawater. When the vessel capsized, numerous openings in the weather deck and deckhouses had not been secured. This created entry points for seawater when the vessel was immersed. These openings were fitted with a means of closure or protection, but they had been left open as the squall approached. Mariners at sea normally secure openings when foul weather approaches. This is something all crew would participate in and is something I would systematically do during my own time on yachts, including during transatlantic crossings in similar conditions to those experienced by the crew on the *Concordia*.

The investigation did not determine why the crew and students did not close the openings (windows and access ways). The investigation did not determine if the crew committed an error or what we call a slip, to conform to scientific research terminology that I use in this book and define further in this chapter. The water entered the hull when it heeled. This compromised the vessel's righting ability to such a degree that it was unable to recover from the knockdown. Downflooding progressed, causing stability to decrease until the vessel finally capsized. If the openings had been secured, the vessel would most likely have righted itself. We all commit errors - slips, lapses, and mistakes. Identifying all of the failures that lead to an accident is a daunting task, an impossible task.

* * *

THE INVESTIGATOR'S MAZE

This recurring feature presents questions specific to the accident that is introduced and is relevant to the theory studied in each chapter, providing some insight into the inquisitive mind of an accident investigator.

When I get a call from the duty officer who has preliminary information about the accident, we engage on a course of action. If I decide that we deploy, the team generally makes its way to the accident site or the port of call of the vessel. We contact and set up interviews with the crew, witnesses, government officials, or a family member - if the vessel is lost at sea.

On the site, we gather data, huge amounts of data, including downloading electronic information such as the voyage data recorder, if there is one. We could plan the data gathering by laying out questions that we need answered. In any event, we would not get all our answers during the interviews, but we give ourselves a base to start the investigation, a canvas to help develop the factual section of the report (a report generally has three sections: factual, analysis, and findings). We will refine and add questions as the investigation unfolds.

Since this chapter is about individual failure, the following is a sample of questions that could be on your mind if you were leading the investigation and wanted to collect data on human error.

· Did they have a plan to deal with foul weather?

· Was the crew rested?

· Did seasickness affect their performance?

· What training did the watch officer have?

· What slips, lapses, and mistakes could have occurred?

* * *

TO ERR IS HUMAN

The loss of the *Concordia* represents the theme of this chapter: individual failure. We make errors every day. Luckily, the vast majority of our miscues have no significant repercussions. Errors that lead to an accident that causes damage to property, personal injury, or loss of life are another story. The only way to prevent these missteps is to understand the truth. This's the tricky part. What is the truth? Finding the cause and contributing factors to an accident requires long hours of investigation and input from experts in various fields. Finding the "real culprit" or "culprits" is a mixture of science, technical abilities, and art. How does the system break down? Why does an accident happen? Why do we fail? More precisely, why does failure exist?

The most obvious answer is that a skill-based performance occurred, such as when an accident occurs between car and pedestrian: *"I did not see him coming… He popped up in front of my car and bang!…*

I was not paying attention to that side of the street." The driver's assessment may not be wrong, but it's also very likely he or she didn't perform the necessary attention checks while driving and was inattentive. Experts call this an inattention failure. Similarly, if a strong habit interferes with the performance of the intended action, this is inattention error, an omitted check, for example, writing the previous year on a cheque in early January? This error occurs when a sequence performed is similar to a more familiar sequence, and the stronger plan of the familiar sequence takes over to control your actions. The outcome may be a habit intrusion, a failure. We all do it. You may have forgotten to perform an attention check at a specific point in an action sequence at your plant or factory.

To understand the origins of the science of error, we must go back to 1881, when the psychologist James Sully published a book on "systematic anomalies or memory, belief, thinking and insight." It remains an obscure read that only some experts refer to. Sigmund Freud, the founder of psychoanalysis, was a contemporary of Sully and read his work. Freud was probably the first to make a theoretical account of slips - improper methods for achieving an objective - dividing them into separate types using a collection of verbal slips that Rudolf Meringer (philologist) and Karl Meyer (psychologist) identified in their 1895 investigation.

The Berlin School of Experimental Psychology researched the probable mechanisms behind our ability to acquire and maintain meaningful perceptions in an apparently chaotic world. When you look at a work environment and try to break it down into small actions and perceptions, it can be overwhelming. The mind forms a global whole with self-organizing tendencies. This central principle is what we call Gestalt psychology, from the German *Gestalt* "shape, form." When the human mind (perceptual system) forms a gestalt, the whole has a reality of its own, independent of the part, per psychologist Kurt Koffka (1935), "The whole is other than the sum of its parts." Gestalt psychologists stipulated that our perceptions are the products of complex interactions among various stimuli. They pursued research to understand the organization of cognitive processes. We do not just collect in our mind simpler and unrelated elements (points, lines, curves, etc.), but we are able to generate whole forms, particularly with respect to the visual recognition of entire figures and scenes. If we want to understand the truth about who may be responsible for errors, we must start by understanding the various slips, lapses, and mistakes we make, at home and at work. These failures are categorized under behavioural groupings.

In today's terminology, we can reinterpret Freud's contribution by separating the two different aspects of cognitive machinery into processing and knowledge. Freud postulated that slips result from competition among underlying mechanisms; they often work in parallel with one another and are generally beneath the consciousness of the individual. The resulting notions are believed to be mental operations controlled by a quasi-hierarchical control structure that activate in parallel with our thoughts and memories, with us being conscious that we access only a limited amount of this activity. We continue today to study and try to explain the differences between conscious and subconscious processing.

If a worker does something he or she did not intend to do, we call this a slip. Slips and lapses occur during skill-based performance where actions tend to be based on stored routines and there is little, if any, conscious decision-making. If a worker has an inappropriate intention to act, we call this a mistake. We make mistakes when we do not choose a proper objective or we carry out an improper method. Mistakes are involved in rule-based performance where decisions are based on learned procedures. Mistakes and adaptations also occur during knowledge-based performance where decisions are based on knowledge and experiences (no set procedures) that necessitate evaluation. Experts separate slips, lapses, and mistakes when the worker intended or did not intend to perform an action that led to a failure. We can categorize, or group, the large collection of slips and observe that they follow patterns.

Professors Donald Arthur Norman and James T. Reason are among the founders of behavioural groupings that list specific modes of failure. They, along with many experts in the area of ergonomics, psychology, and human factors, made significant contributions to the field of human error. Professor Norman is a leader in the fields of design, usability engineering, and cognitive science. He was part of a team that investigated the Three Mile Island nuclear accident, an accident that I relate in the opening of Chapter II. Reason was a professor of psychology at the University of Manchester when he wrote his book *Human Error*, now a reference in the field of theories on occupational accidents. He is also renowned for his work in the areas of perception, cognitive psychology, human and organizational factors in complex systems, and for his extensive research of the psychology of human error. I cover his theory (his model) of error in the next chapter.

FAILURE MODES

"(An error is) a generic term to encompass all those occasions in which a planned sequence of mental or physical activities fails to achieve its intended outcome, and when these failures cannot be attributed to the intervention of some chance agency." (James Reason, 1990)

The following is an inexhaustive explanation of failure modes, the variety of failures. It separates errors into slips, lapses, and mistakes, provides definitions of each, and also gives examples from everyday life that will help readers understand that we're all prone to failure whether we realize it or not. It should be noted, however, that while most of our daily mishaps, whether at home or in the community, have inconsequential effect or minor negative impact, a similar failure mode performed in the workplace can lead to devastating consequences.

WAS THAT A SLIP OR A LAPSE?

We all slip. We all do unintentional actions. We fail because we were not attentive, or not attentive enough. We commit execution errors that we call a slip. We lapse when we execute errors that involve an unintentional action because of a memory failure. The link between a slip and a lapse is the unintentional action. The difference between a slip and a lapse is the error in attention or memory. We commit many different types of slips and lapses that experts place under the behaviour grouping called skill-based performance errors. This failure mode comprises the following skill-based performance errors.

Do you remember that time when you were unpacking a new item you purchased and you threw the item in the bin and kept the packaging in your hands? It was either an ambiguity and/or distractions that interfered with your performance. You did the correct action, but on the wrong object. This slip could happen when your internal description of the intended action is not sufficiently precise. The more wrong and right objects have in common, like physical location, the more likely the error is to occur. Do you remember having misplaced your car keys at the same place you put your wallet? You can induce this failure if you are distracted, bored, preoccupied, under stress, or otherwise not inclined to pay full attention.

We can omit to do things if interrupted at the time we should take action. The interruption causes the failure at a critical time, a moment planned as an attention check. While monitoring the cooking of your dinner, you plan to check on the food and start the vegetables at the 15-minute mark, but your child arrives and calls you for assistance. The interruption focuses your mind away from cooking. When you return to the kitchen, at the 15-minute mark, you check the food but forget to put the heat on under the vegetable pot. Later, when you check on the food, you find that you forgot to cook the vegetables.

We omit to do things regularly when interrupted. However, when our omission is part of a series of critical events, it can be disastrous. It is easy to imagine ourselves crashing our cars as we answer an upsetting call on our cellphone. This is exactly what happened on July 7, 2010, and was the cause of a fatal accident on the Delaware River in Philadelphia, PA. A tugboat was towing an empty sludge barge when it collided with a small passenger vessel at anchor. One cause of this accident was the failure of the mate on the tug to maintain a proper lookout, omitting to do his main duty. He was distracted and inattentive due to repeated personal use of his cellphone and company laptop computer while being solely responsible for navigating the vessel. Two passengers were killed aboard the passenger vessel and 26 others suffered minor injuries.

We can all recall a recent time when we did something along the lines of the following mishap. You leave the basement in your home and enter the kitchen, only to wonder why you are there. Your mind wandered when you left the basement; you focused on matters other than the reason why you were making your way to the kitchen. In order to remember why we are where we are, we generally backtrack to where we were when we left to be where we now are. If there is a delay between the formulation of an intended action and the time you take action, and you do not carry out the appropriate attention checks, other demands may overlay the intended action. Fundamentally, three things happen. First, there is a delay between your planned action and its execution. Second, you do not make the appropriate attention checks. Finally, your actions initiated by other demands replace the intended action.

During routine tasks, you may select an object that you accept for another object because it looks like the intended object, it is in the expected location, and/or it does a similar job. Just think about putting baking soda rather than baking powder in your recipe when both ingredients are side by side in the same cupboard. How many times have you mistaken the hair conditioner for the shampoo? Have you ever picked up the wrong clicker in the television room? These three examples are similar in that they are routine actions for you, there is a rough approximation accepted for the real object, and the objects look alike, they are in the expected location, and/or do a similar job as the intended object you wanted to use.

You can pay too much attention - be on over attention - and therefore either omit, repeat, or reverse an action. You may attend to the progress of an action sequence at the wrong time. This can result in the assessment that the process is further along than it actually is, and, therefore, you can omit an essential step in the sequence. You set the kettle to boil water. Just as you check the status of the boiling water, you realize it is hot enough and pour it into the teapot without inserting the tea bag. You may omit a step, or you may repeat a step. Let us say you put the water on to boil. You then put a tea bag in the teapot a minute after checking if the temperature of the water is right. During a second check, you inadvertently put a second tea bag in the teapot.

In another situation, you have a checklist. You are going over steps one by one. You get interrupted from your work. When you get back to your job, you resume the checklist at the wrong place and reset a previously set switch. Rather than consciously turning a system on, you moved the selector from where it is to "where it is not." Mistimed checks can cause an action sequence to double back on itself. You inappropriately timed your check of a bidirectional action sequence and reversed the action sequence.

A (NOT SO) SIMPLE MISTAKE

You make a mistake when you intend to do something. You have an intended action. You made a bad plan. You made an error because you made an error in planning. Your mistake was intentional, but you did not deliberately decide to act against a rule or a plan. In this case, experts say they are rule-based failures or plan-based performance failures. It applies to errors when you are making familiar decisions using stored rules, such as "if I see this condition" then "I take this action." You would make an error because either you misclassified the condition, which resulted in you taking an incorrect action, or because you just took the incorrect action. You failed because you misapplied a good rule or you applied a bad rule.

You may make a mistake because you apply a rule you have used frequently in the past, but it is incorrect for the situation. For Canadian or US citizens that visit each other's country for the first time, this could mean applying the metric system rather than the imperial system (or vice-versa). We fill the gas tank in either litres or gallons, we travel in miles per hour or kilometres per hour, etc. It can therefore be easy to misapply a speed limit rule if the signage only puts a number.

The strength of a rule depends on the number of times you successfully applied it. The more successful you are in applying a rule, the stronger the rule becomes ingrained in your mind. The stronger the rule is ingrained, the more likely you will choose it, even when the match between the situation and the rule is not adequate. During my training as a hovercraft pilot, I learned that the critical point where I was likely to have my first accident is at 25 hours of flying time. I had to be careful, as I would be applying the same rules - the same techniques - successfully for a period of time sufficient to cause the rules to become ingrained and then I may apply these rules in another similar situation that would warrant another rule, another technique. I would become comfortable applying the same technique that had successfully worked for the previous 25 hours of flying time.

Depending on where you live in the world, you drive on the right or the left. If you visit another country, the United Kingdom, for example, if you are a North American citizen, you would be driving on the other side. You could easily apply a general rule error coming out of the driveway of the car rental company, driving on the wrong side, because you have ingrained its frequency of occurrence. Another example, you borrow a friend's pickup truck in order to move in a different city. It starts pouring rain. You need to locate the switch or control system for the wipers. You continue attending to your driving and look to see if the tarpaulin is holding up and preventing the rain from drenching the couch and the mattress. You are understandably in a stressful situation. You may apply an incorrect rule because of the overwhelming amount of information confronting you. The result, in this situation, may be that you activate the high-beam lights rather than the wipers.

Now, imagine it is the first time you encounter a significant exception to a general rule that has been very reliable in the past. You may continue to "rule" in your mind. You chose an incorrect general rule for the situation because you find it difficult to make the first-time choice of the correct alternative. You can also stick to a method of carrying out a task since you have been successful at doing it in the past. You strongly believe in the correctness of the method despite the presence of more appropriate options. You need to redesign the task before you fail.

Engineers, with the help of technicians, develop equipment that can enable more actions than it has controls or displays. The operator may select the wrong mode that, if unchecked, can lead to an accident. For example, electronics such as iPods have buttons that have more than one application. If the controls are required to do more than one function and the equipment does not provide visible mode change (side press buttons, for example, for accessing a menu and for scrolling up and down), the information provided to the operator can be ambiguous and mode errors ensue. The user is unsure of the mode status of the equipment and selects inappropriate actions.

Rules may also contain weaknesses or a defect in the intended implementation strategy. We see an amber light and we increase speed in order to advance through an intersection. The amber light is a cautionary signal. It is bad logic to assume one always has a clear safe path. If you accelerate, you commit a wrong rule error because the plan of the rule is flawed.

We can employ solutions that are clumsy, circuitous, or weird. Because they work, they can become established as part of our rule-based procedures. We investigated numerous accidents where operators had jury-rigged a piece of equipment in lieu of obtaining a *bona fide* part, or used a tool to bypass or override a system. Without the benefit of expert instructions to the contrary and because it was working, operating in a forgiving environment, workers continued using the temporary fix. However, these solutions eventually and usually fail. An inefficient rule flourishes because checks within the operating environment do not exist or have not functioned properly.

For example, a tractor operator at a golf course takes off his helmet to relieve himself from the heat it generates. He was out of the way, or so he thought, of the incoming golf balls from the adjacent hole he was tasked to maintain. A ball flies by his head, barely missing him. Although the inadvisable rule may be adequate to achieve its immediate goal and you can get away with it most of the time, continuing to use it in the long run is inadvisable because it can lead to avoidable accidents. The inadvisable rule violates established codes or operating procedures, and, in the end, the activity can result in an accident. Although the rule works, there is high accident risk associated with its use and the rule breaches established procedures, standards, etc.

POORLY ADAPTED PLANS... OFTEN GO AWRY

We find solutions or formulate plans when we want to solve problems to given situations where no rules apply. If we commit an error during the formulation of the solutions or plans, we are making knowledge-based performance mistakes.

We can make mistakes intentionally without deliberately acting against a rule or a plan. We can also fail when we deliberately decide to act against a rule or a plan. We can fail during routine adaptations, such as when we modify or do not strictly comply with work procedures because of poorly designed or poorly defined work practices. We can also fail during an exceptional adaptation, a one-time breach of a work practice, such as when we deliberately ignore a safety test.

You can pay attention to the wrong characteristics or you do not pay attention to the right characteristics. Your engine fault light is on. You focus your attention to physically salient symptoms and look for noise, heat, and smell. You focus on physically important characteristics or evidence. You look at brightness and loudness. You look at what is centrally visible and what you can easily interpret. You do not find the true nature of the fault. You ignore critical cues that provide diagnostic information about the nature of a problem. You ignore other critical cues, such as driver input and forgo using instruments to diagnose the problem. You do not process all information available to you. This is often compounded under times of stress.

You may also seek information that will confirm what you already believe to be true. You then ignore or discount other information because it is inconsistent with the chosen hypothesis. You pay attention only to give information that supports a hypothesis you previously chose. We can choose to discount information because it is not consistent with our chosen hypothesis.

When you have to make a risky decision, you tend to frame your problem as a choice between gains or between losses. With respect to losses, you are biased and choose the risky loss, which is less probable although more disastrous, than the certain loss. For example, when returning home from a visit to a foreign country, you may have chosen not to declare the unauthorized second bottle of 20-year-old Scotch to avoid paying duty. If you initially claim to the border guard that you have a second bottle, you know the amount to pay - it is small, but you will lose time at the border. If the guard discovers your second bottle, the unknown cost (risky loss) may be higher, but you consider it less likely to occur. You rated your alternatives on the airplane in terms of losses (or gains) and made a decision between the choices of a sure loss versus an uncertain probability of higher impact. Generally, people are biased toward the risky choice which can lead to an accident in a work environment.

People tend to overestimate the correctness of their knowledge of the situation and its outcome. You can place attention only on information that supports your choice and you ignore contra-dictory evidence. You overrate your knowledge of the situation. A common scenario for this occurs with inexperienced and newly trained employees. They can fall prey to this bias when they attempt to apply their training. Since they have not been tempered with on-the-job experience, they overrate the utility of their classroom theory. They should have relied more on workshop-oriented knowledge used by their co-workers. If you do not recall this type of mistake, you may remember the time you splatted paint on the wall after you quickly raised your arm with the paintbrush you just dipped in paint. There was too much paint, you moved quickly, or you were just plain clumsy while learning a new skill. Someone had told you this may happen, but you did not listen and did not emulate the more experienced painter.

We often resort to "mental rules of thumb" to help diagnose a problem without expending too much mental effort and, hence, too much time. We often resort to these heuristics because they serve us well. Nevertheless, they are shortcuts and, as such, you may be shortchanging yourself of adequate and accurate information. If you take a shortcut, you may give yourself a false understanding of the actual situation since you did not process all available infor-mation and you did not follow reasoning to its most probable and logical conclusion.

You may be comparing information you perceive with what exists in your memory. It is a tendency that we have to match cues drawn from a current situation to those that form a mental representation of a particular situation that already exists in our long-term memory. If you decide that the cues of the current situation match those of a particular situation stored in your memory, then you may draw a conclusion that the situations are similar or identical. In turn, you may conclude the action you had taken previously is also appropriate to apply at this time. However, if the cues you perceive from the current situation were not complete or were ambiguous, you can conclude on an incorrect match. Should the pattern of cues in your long-term memory not be a good indicator of the current situation, then your judgment and decision-making could be faulty.

Once people establish a match, they tend to cling to that interpretation, often not changing it despite evidence to the contrary. As an example, just recall the last time you asked for direction in an area you already visited a few times. You rolled down the window of your car and inquired with a person who happened to be very loquacious. They mention a few street names and landmarks that sound familiar. From memory, you make a mental map of your route. You somehow discarded the other directional cues. The result is that your mental map was not very great and you got lost again. You perceived information that you incorrectly matched with specific patterns stored in your memory. Therefore, you improperly interpreted the current situation and took incorrect actions.

We also have a tendency to diagnose a situation using the hypothesis most available in memory. We give undue weight to facts that come readily to mind. The most available hypothesis may not be the most probable, but simply one recently experienced or the lesser complicated one that comes to mind. Someone shows you a picture with a pattern of lines and asks you what you think it is. It takes you a few minutes and you cannot recall what the pattern represents. Then you are told that it is a map of a coastal area. When you are shown another picture, you see the pattern of lines in terms of another map. As it turned out, the pattern was an outline of a dog's head. You selected an inappropriate hypothesis because of its convenience.

Finally, you can incorrectly perceive all the information with the same weighting of reliability. For example, personally, I am not too good at taking measurements. My usage of a measuring tape will most likely not render the same result as you. In fact, I need the new electronic gadget that calculates the distance using laser technology, less fallible. We can use several methods and technologies to measure; all have their intrinsic level of precision. However, we have a tendency to treat all information sources "as if" they were of equal reliability. You may be considering information that is, at best, marginal, as having the same degree of reliability as that which is very reliable. If you are like me, you do not get the exact same length of the plank depending on the tool you use to measure. You may give the same weight of reliability to both instruments. Professionals do not seem to need electronics. Perhaps you and I should use more reliable instruments and not give the same weight to manual and laser technology.

AT FIRST GLANCE

An Uber autonomous vehicle did not stop and killed a 49-year-old woman crossing the street in 2017. After the accident, the Associated Press reported that the chief of police in Tempe, AZ, had indicated that it was not the vehicle's fault. Two experts who saw the video of the fatal accident believed otherwise. The lidar (laser detection and ranging) and radar should have detected Mrs. Herzberg and her bicycle in time to stop. The vehicle is to blame. Lidars and radars can see in darkness, much better than humans and cameras. The victim was well within the range of these systems. Further, with the help of the video that was recording the driver, it seemed clear that driver was relying too much on the autonomous systems. She was not watching the road.

This story illustrates the adage that if everyone is responsible, then nobody is. The local police posted the video in the hope of helping its investigators determine all responsible in this accident. Nevertheless, without taking time to examine all the facts, the chief of police stated, shortly after the accident, that we should not blame the autonomous vehicle, essentially telling us that the victim was crossing the street outside the pedestrian crossing area. It is very clear, the chief of police said to the *San Francisco Chronicle*, that it would have been very difficult to avoid a collision whatever the mode of the vehicle given that the victim was coming out of the shadow and ended up straight on the road. So, who is to blame? Is anyone to blame? Or is this simply a case where we all make mistakes in normal day-to-day actions?

Any given action sequence in the workplace or even in our daily life chores is usually quite complex. There are a large number of components involved, multiple intentions, plans, and a considerable time devoted to some simple tasks. Performing a workplace task or daily life chore properly requires appropriate triggering conditions. We are easily subject to slips, lapses, mistakes, and we are often poor at adapting plans.

HUMAN PERFORMANCE, NOT ALWAYS UP TO PAR

Human reliability relates to human factors and ergonomics. Both are scientific pillars in the field of industrial accidents, as well as other fields such as medicine. We commit slips, lapses, and mistakes that affect the resilience of the systems. Our performance is affected by our age, our physical health, our attitudes, our emotions, and our general state of mind. It is also affected by contextually induced variables such as noise, humidity, vibration, and temperature. People are a crucial component of large socio-technical systems. When we fail, the system fails.

We all tend to overestimate our ability to maintain control when we work. We may recognize that we are stressed, but we may underestimate the impact of stress as it creeps stealthily upon us and affects our ability to perform, especially because stress is cumulative. Homo sapiens do not like to put much effort into high-level attention tasks for extended periods; we are reluctant to spend much time concentrating. We often use mental shortcuts to expedite decision-making. This also can lead to failure. Our mind's short-term memory, where we conduct problem solving and decision-making, has limits. We do not have a great attention span. In fact, we have a limited ability to concentrate on two or more activities at a time, which challenges our ability to process information needed to solve problems.

We tend to focus more on what we want to accomplish and less on the things we avoid. We are primarily goal-oriented by nature and see what our minds expect or want us to see. Emotion and fatigue can also affect our reliability as we are all susceptible to emotional and social factors such as anger and embarrassment. Each of us has experienced these adverse feelings individually or as part of a team. We all get tired or can be tired as we arrive to work, and physical, emotional, and mental fatigue can lead to errors and poor judgment. Finally, some employees will be at the workplace in a diminished capacity due to illness or injury. It is not enough to determine why someone committed an error, but we also need to look at why the unsafe act was performed by the human operator on the front line.

We find workers making individual errors well before and immediately prior to accidents and disasters. We cannot change the fact that you and every worker fails. In fact, some authors (Conlin, 2012) claim that workers can commit as many as seven errors per hour. It is likely that someone will say a slip, a lapse, or a mistake created a disaster, but that alone is not the sole cause or contributing factor. There are sufficient checks and balances in the transportation system and in every highly sophisticated industry to prevent an individual from being the unique person at fault.

We continue to examine processes, operational procedures, laws and regulations to uncover trouble before trouble finds us. This is why governments and industry investigate accidents. Procedures, processes, and techniques nowadays abound and the system is generally robust. But errors do happen and this is why we continue to be interested in how we create and operate work environments, and why, by necessity, understanding failure is crucial to the safety of every individual and success of any organization.

CLOSING ARGUMENTS

Everyone fails when a workplace accident happens; every party near to far who participates in the creation of a work environment participates in its failure. We all make errors and we all lie about them whether we are conscious of doing so or not. Why? The reasons are myriad and can often distract from the investigation.

Too often, we fall into the trap of searching for a guilty party or a quick explanation when an accident occurs, rather than focusing on the cause, which can take months and years of painstaking work.

When an 80-metre section of the Morandi Bridge in Genoa, Italy, collapsed one morning in August 2018, killing 43 people and leaving hundreds homeless, officials took to cast blame on poor infrastructure maintenance and promising that the responsible parties "would pay" (Giuffrida, 2018). This while sniffer dogs were still combing the rubble in the hopes of locating survivors. Why? Searching for the guilty party is the inevitable focus when a disaster hits. In fact, most people have a tendency to fixate on a single party or single cause for a disaster. The blame often falls on the last person to cope with the consequences of the accident-enabling behaviour, such as those last to touch the structure, the maintenance team. Captains, pilots, and plant shift workers are also often scapegoats. However, as we will see in the next chapter, when it comes to disasters, there is never a single-point failure.

The occurrence may have had minimal consequences, or it may have had disastrous effects - killing hundreds, ruining the environment, costing millions, and even creating a crisis. Nevertheless, we cannot stop ourselves from looking for quick answers, forgoing the long analysis required to finding out why. Regardless of the effort and scrutiny required to finalize an investigation, we jump to conclusions and oversimplify the result. In the case of the *Concordia*, for example, it would have been facile to point to the capricious nature of the sea as the main culprit behind the loss of the vessel and endangerment of lives. Experts agreed. Further analysis, however, revealed the fingerprints of human involvement in the accident.

Investigators must find out if a person, a system, or the government is at fault in order to understand what led to an accident. They are not searching for a party to blame albeit this is somewhat of a semantic debate. When they find fault, many say they are blaming. In fact, they are searching for ways to prevent the accident from happening again. Blaming is a negative side effect of the findings, a public spin given to attract attention and sell the story.

We are all interested in knowing that our modes of transportation and our work environments are safe. We are surely all interested in preventing further accidents from occurring in our workplaces and in our lives. We should therefore all be interested in understanding the why behind failure, more so than the who. This brings us to the next chapter. We will show you that the culprit can also be a system, a policy or a work environment.

II

Beyond the Usual Suspects
The Long List of Contributors to an Accident

LOOKING FOR CLUES

> › *Multiple-point failures*
>
> › *How accidents are theorized*
>
> › *The dawn of determinism*
>
> › *The reason for reasoning*
>
> › *Putting theories into practice*
>
> › *Work-as-done versus work-as-imagined*

Sam arrived at the Three Mile Island nuclear complex in Pennsylvania on the morning of March 28, 1979, well rested after a good night's sleep. Good thing. He was the lead of a team of workers relieving the night shift and facing a problem that occurred overnight that was left undiagnosed and led to major reactor damage and an emergency call. Sam and his team would detect the problem, owing, in part, to a different and fresh mindset, and prevent a large-scale disaster. What follows is a simplified explanation of the technical and scientific details of the event.

In the hours preceding the incident, one reactor at the facility was running at 97 percent power. The companion reactor was being refuelled and was not operational. In the early morning one of the three main water/steam loops in a pressurized water reactor began to malfunction. However, the initial trigger started 11 hours earlier. The operators were attempting to fix a blockage in one of eight condensate polishers, which are sophisticated filters that clean the secondary loop water. Blockages are common with filters, including these. The operators were having difficulties cleaning them and decided to blow compressed air into the water and let the force clear the filters. In doing so, a small amount of water forced its way past a check valve that was stuck open, eventually causing the pumps to turn off, resulting in a turbine trip.

Heat and pressure then increased in the reactor coolant system. The reactor continued to generate decay (damaging) heat and, because steam was no longer being used by the turbine, heat was no longer being removed from the reactor's primary water loop. Three auxiliary pumps activated automatically. However, the system was unable to pump water since the valves were closed for routine maintenance! The problems did not end there.

A relief valve opened automatically. It should have closed, but it got stuck open because of a mechanical fault. A light on the control panel indicated that the valve was closed. The operators were not able to correctly diagnose the problem for several hours. The open valve permitted coolant water to escape from the primary system. This was the principal mechanical cause of the primary coolant system depressurization.

There were other problems. The design of the relief valve indicator light was flawed: No light was supposed to mean the valve was shut, whereas, in fact, it was stuck open. When everything was operating correctly, the indicator light was true and the operators relied on it. The valve being stuck open and the light off confused the operators. The instruments showed the pressure, temperature, and coolant levels in the primary circuit as behaving improperly. However, the operators were unable to determine with certainty what was happening, even after considering different scenarios according to the readings. Ultimately, they were unable to break out of a cycle of assumptions. Then Sam and the day shift team arrived with a fresh pot of coffee and a different mindset. Unfortunately, by this time, the major damage leading to a partial core meltdown had already occurred. Sam and his team could not prevent it from happening.

The operators were not trained to understand the ambiguous nature of the valve indicator. They did not know to look for alternative confirmation that the main relief valve was closed. The temperature indicator downstream showed that the temperature was higher than it should have been. However, this indicator was not part of the safety procedure and was located out of the sight of the operators.

The overall water level inside the pressurizer was rising. There was no dedicated instrument to measure the level of water in the core. The operators judged the level of water in the core solely by the level in the pressurizer. It was high, so they assumed that the core was properly covered with coolant. Unfortunately, again, the indicator provided misleading readings because of steam forming in the reactor vessel. Indications of high-water levels contributed to the confusion. The operators were taught to be concerned about the lack of a steam pocket buffer existing in the pressurizer. The operators did not recognize that the core lacked coolant. They turned off the emergency core cooling pumps, which had automatically started after the relief valve got stuck. This would lead to the loss of coolant.

The pressurizer relief tank overfilled. An alarm sounded, indicating that there was an ongoing loss of coolant. The operators ignored this. Shortly after, a relief diaphragm on the pressurizer relief tank ruptured, and the radioactive coolant began to leak into the general containment building. A couple hours later, the top of the reactor core was exposed. The intense heat caused a reaction to occur that melted the nuclear fuel rod cladding and damaged the fuel pellets. In turn, radioactive isotopes released in the reactor coolant and produced hydrogen gas. The investigation determined that this could have resulted in a small explosion. When contaminated water reached detectors, radiation detectors activated, sounding alarms. The radiation levels in the primary coolant water were around 300 times normal levels. The general containment building was seriously contaminated. Richard, the plant supervisor, declared a site area emergency. The core melted and the general containment building was seriously contaminated.

In 1984, Charles Perrow, a professor of sociology and the author of several books and numerous articles on understanding the socio-logical impacts of large organizations, became one of the first scientists to determine that work environments are systems that can lead to accidents. He concluded that the failure at Three Mile Island was a consequence of the system's immense complexity. Such modern high-risk systems, he realized, were prone to failures. This is true even for well-managed work environments. It was inevitable that the nuclear plant would eventually suffer - what Perrow termed - a normal accident. Therefore, he suggested that we might do better to contemplate a radical redesign or, if that was not possible, abandon such technology entirely.

Normal accidents, or system accidents, are so called by Perrow because such accidents are inevitable in extremely complex systems. Given the characteristics of the system, multiple failures that interact will inevitably occur, despite efforts to avoid them. Such events appear trivial to begin with, but unpredictably cascade through the system until they create a large event with severe consequences. These accidents occur as a result of an unanti-cipated interaction of multiple failures in a complex system. Three Mile Island was an example of this type of accident. Staff could not comprehend, control, or avoid it. So, *whodunit*? Who can be responsible for "normal" accidents?

I chose the story of Three Mile Island to open the chapter dedicated to accident theories because it is generally known as the event that initiated the creation of my former professional field of investiga-tions. This nuclear disaster led to the proliferation of workplace accident theories and key intellectual concepts. Perrow started to revolutionize the concept of safety and risk. Three Mile Island set the standard for examining technological failures as the product of highly complex and interactive systems and highlighted organ-izational and management factors as the main causes of a system breakdown. We could no longer ascribe technological disasters to isolated equipment malfunction, operator error, or "acts of God." From then on, we had to change the way we perceived the genesis of accidents and disasters.

We now know that searching for a guilty party means identifying multiple parties. Failure is a system failure. There is no such thing as identifying a single-source failure. Disasters are the result of many decisions, interactions, and actions. Failure is the result of social and technical decisions made by a long list of people, organizations, and even governments, lobbyists, and concerned citizens.

The operators, a team consisting of engineers and technicians, were busy carrying out their normal duties and responsibilities, oblivious to the fact that things were starting to go wrong at Three Mile Island. The nuclear reactor eventually melted down and caused major disruption and confusion. Fortunately, it was more of a wake-up call than creating health or safety impacts to the surrounding community and state. Perrow and other contemporary scholars carried out the groundwork on how we should conduct proper investigations. Today, investigators use various accident causation theories to understand failure in the work environment. With these theories, investigators develop techniques, methodologies, and models to identify failure. This is what I will explain next, which will position us to understand how investigators use theory to identify the people, systems, policies, and environment that were conducive to creating the accident.

* * *

THE INVESTIGATOR'S MAZE

I remind you that this feature presents questions specifically to the accident that is introduced and is relevant to the theory studied in each chapter, providing some insight into the inquisitive mind of an accident investigator.

In the first maze, I identified questions about human error. I explained that we collect data; we start doing this when we receive preliminary information about an occurrence that leads to the launch of an investigation. The investigator-in-charge and his/her team collect large amounts of data at the site of the occurrence, and they continue doing this until the report is published. Back at the office, the team organizes the data. They place the information, albeit often fragmentary, into the context of an occurrence sequence. The investigation takes on another life.

The investigation team starts digging further into the event, examining the players, the systems and the environments. They try to identify unsafe acts, poor decisions and unsafe conditions with the ultimate goal to identify safety problems. They end up with more questions and the need for more data. The investigator-in-charge goes to the owners of this information and makes a verbal or written request. Uncooperative owners will receive a statutory summons which forces them to produce information or records. In some situations, a judge could sign a warrant to search and seize, and on many occasions a statutory summons is issued to compel reluctant witnesses to attend an interview.

In any case, if you are investigating an event such as the Three Mile Island, you request way more information and do more interviews with front-line workers, managers, decision-makers, family members, suppliers, government, etc. You come up with a game plan that can be laid out in the form of questions.

· Do we have all the plans of the nuclear power plant?

· Do we have all the procedures, checklists, and operational manuals?

· Did we interview all the decision-makers, including the line managers?

· Do we need to request information from some manufacturers?

· Is this a situation of multi-point failures?

* * *

THE LONG LIST OF CULPRITS

Captain Francesco Schettino is serving 16 years in prison for manslaughter. He was the master of the cruise ship *Costa Concordia* that grounded and capsized off the coast of Italy, killing 33 people in June 2012. The operator, Carnival, a subsidiary of Coast Cruises, escaped relatively unscathed. The company had nothing to do with this disaster, according to the Italian judiciary system. The enforcement officers examined the crew's decisions to determine if they were hasty, measured, or ill-informed. By contrast, the same scrutiny was not applied to the companies and governments that have the true power to change safety practices and culture. Too bad, Captain Schettino, society wants blood, and you were it: the unique culprit, and the scapegoat for the *Costa Concordia* disaster.

The Italian government launched several investigations into the accident, including a no-blame investigation aimed at finding causes and contributing factors. The captain was responsible, but there were other "culprits." The report submitted to both the European Union and the International Maritime Organization is based on accident causation theory, the topic of this chapter. Finding all the "guilty" parties requires much work. Finding all the "guilty" parties means forgetting about revenge, discounting first impressions, and putting emotions aside. Can this be done? Shouldn't we be concerned with finding all the failures in the system? Do we really think that Schettino intended to run the vessel aground? Of course not.

When an accident occurs, something has gone wrong in the functioning of the socio-technical system. Everyday accidents can take benign forms, such as machinery breakdowns, or can lead to tragic events, such as a death in the workplace. Localized accidents, such as an employee falling off a ladder and sustaining a small injury, happen in unidentifiable numbers. Finding the causes and contributing factors that led the employee to fall might be easy. However, the fall could also involve multiple factors that warrant close examination. This includes examining the ladder itself; determining if safety procedures exist or not and, if so, scrutinizing their quality; studying the level of fatigue of the employee(s); investigating if the employees were pressured to carry out the job, etc. The lines of query can grow ever larger in scope until the magnitude of a seemingly simple investigation becomes enormous.

Accident investigators looked at the *Costa Concordia* accident comprehensively. Teams may determine that their search for the truth requires a major level of effort. It may be apparent that getting to the root causes and finding the truth requires identifying all the facts and analyzing the complex forms and interactions of many levels of industry, government, and civil society.

An event that was thoroughly investigated is the Lac-Mégantic (Quebec) train disaster. It occurred just before 11:00 p.m. on July 5, 2013, when a Montreal, Maine & Atlantic Railway train arrived at Nantes, QC, carrying 7.7 million litres of petroleum crude oil in 72 Class 111 tank cars. Originating in New Town, North Dakota, the train was bound for Saint John, New Brunswick. Almost all of the 63 derailed tank cars were damaged, and many had large breaches. About six million litres of oil were quickly released, and a fire began almost immediately. The ensuing blaze and explosions left 47 people dead. Another 2,000 were forced from their homes, and much of the downtown core of the community was destroyed.

Each investigation body crafts their own report template, usually to reflect home legislation or applicable International Convention related to the mode of transportation. Investigation reports normally include three sections: factual, analysis, and findings. The findings can comprise causes, contributing factors, recommendations, and risks. Causes and contributing factors are extracted from the analysis section to summarize the multiple failure points. For the purpose of keeping with the story thread of this essay, you identify all the "culprits." Risks do not necessarily lead directly to the accident, they are related unsafe acts, unsafe conditions, or safety issues with the potential to degrade safety.

The chain of events that led to this disaster is not limited to the engineer who inappropriately applied the hand brakes. The investigation found 18 causes and contributing factors, and 16 risks. In this case, as in so many disasters, identifying causes and contributing factors requires examination of numerous human factors, including those at the economic, political, sociological, organizational, and individual level. You need a methodology to be able to properly identify the factors that need attention. There is no standard template or model for doing this. There is no standard investigation technique or investigation model since there is no such thing as a typical accident. Before selecting a methodology to conduct your investigation, you need to understand how and why accidents happen. You need a theory (you need a model) or, as we will see, several theories. Once you understand how accidents are created, you can then create an investigation methodology to uncover all of the causes, contributing factors, and risks.

The rail accident created many questions, among them: was the locomotive engineer responsible? After all, as the investigation revealed, he had not applied sufficient hand brakes before leaving the train for the night on top of a low-grade hill with 72 tank cars full of highly volatile petroleum products. How about the owner: was he responsible? The train owner tried to get everyone to believe he had nothing to do with it. Anne-Marie Saint-Cerny, an environmental activist, in her book, *Une tragédie annoncée*, believes otherwise. I imagine by now, if you have read the previous sections of this book, you probably understand why she also does not believe there was a single-point failure.

Saint-Cerny claims that the owner of the railway hired a CEO upon taking financial control of the company. The pair put in place a plan to cut costs and make it a more profitable endeavour to satisfy shareholders. One of the decisions of the pair was to put "one-man crews" on their trains. Convoys would increase in length and load, while equipment and rails would wear out without government intervention. Saint-Cerny reveals what was already known in many industries in the western world, industries may compromise safety to increase profits. She repeats in her book the obvious government claim that railroad companies are responsible for the security of their infrastructure, their material, and their operations (Saint-Cerny, 2018). Therefore, an owner and a CEO would be responsible for safety. They could also be blamed for an accident. I prefer to say that they participated in the overall failures that led to the disaster. Investigators do not like to blame or search for guilty parties. Investigators search for what broke down in the system.

The courts did not send the train conductor to jail. When you dig and investigate, you find that the Lac-Mégantic derailment was a disaster in the making. I am not aware of how Saint-Cerny conducted her investigative journalism, but investigators that produced the independent government report used a methodology based on accident causation theory. The investigators built a case and wrote a report centred on technical methods sourced from their understanding of the work conducted by accident causation scientists, and there are few in this field. Scientists have developed theoretical models to help understand and explain what happened, to help find all the culprits, so to speak. If you want to play the blame game of identifying all the "culprits" in a large disaster or very serious accidents such as the explosion of the space shuttle *Challenger*, be ready to identify everyone who was involved or knew something from a long way back. I will show you why.

ACCIDENT THEORIES ABOUND

The main theoretical accident causation models can either help understand how a complete industrial system broke down or help identify individual failure that contributed to an accident. Work systems are complex, comprising vast interactions and various components of safety. There could also be, of course, the absence of safety components. When an accident happens, it is never because of only one factor (active failure or dangerous act), but it is the result of multiple latent factors that already existed in the work area and/or a combination of several human and technical failures. It is therefore essential that we use good theoretical models to understand the complexity of the relationships involved in the work environment. Of course, if you are only interested in understanding the impact of one factor (e.g., breakdown of an engine component) or one actor (e.g., a slip), then you do not need to understand the theoretical models of accident causation. However, if you are interested in improving safety and want to understand why the engine broke down and why the worker committed a slip, then you need a comprehensive approach to your investigation.

In order to develop a holistic approach and grasp how workers conduct their tasks in a complex system, one must understand two aspects of what causes all accidents. The first is the various dynamics between people, policies, and their work environments. The second is the dynamic interactions, the vulnerabilities, and the factors at play when the worker is placed at the centre of the work environment.

Many authors have devised theoretical models to explain accidents. We generally classify them in three categories: sequential (simple linear model), epidemiological (complex linear model), and systemic (non-linear). Sequential models put emphasis on the causal chain of events. The archetype of a simplistic sequential model is Heinrich's (1931) Domino model *(see Figure 1)*. This theory postulates that a sequence of factors leads to an accident. The accident happened because of an unsafe act carried out by a person and/or a mechanical or physical hazard. The system was stable until it was disturbed. We can devise sequential models using event fault trees that describe a series of actions.

Epidemiological theories consider the structural causes of an accident more globally, although, as in all theories, the dual objective and subjective relationships that occur in an accident at work are difficult to measure. We say epidemiological models are complex linear models because we describe the accident as the result of a series of logical combinations of conditions. We use a fault tree. The easy way to remember the difference between an event tree and a fault tree is that the latter organizes the accident with binary branching trees as opposed to events (dominoes).

Fig. 1

Systemic theories do not focus on the causal chain, but rather on the uncontrollable variables in the system that have harmed or hindered the performance of the work system. Because major accidents involve complex concurrences of multiple factors, we need a model that describes the dynamic bindings that resulted in the accident. We need to understand how the dynamic stability resulted in instability. We need to describe concurrence. We need to describe a system. This requires strong multi-disciplinary investigation teams, lots of creativity and lots of sweat, something that governments have in short supply given workload and the allocation of scarce resources. Investigators do not use any specific systemic theory to develop their investigation model for accidents such as the Lac-Mégantic train disaster. Rather, they start with a model that uses epidemiological theories to lay out the areas of research and then they study the dynamic bindings - the performance - as individual components that led to the accident.

The two most commonly used theoretical models in occupational accidents are epidemiological models, namely the SHELL and James Reason's (1990) Accident Causation and generic error-modelling system (GEMS) frameworks models. I will spend a bit of time on these and will also explain a very interesting theoretical model that is absent from the practitioners' toolbox, the sociological accident model of Tom Dwyer, a model that does not fall into any of the three categories. The sociological accident model is helpful for understanding the complexities of developing workable systemic models when you want to investigate the social dynamics that lead to an accident. It is also a model to understand some dynamic bindings (e.g., pressure to produce a greater output of widgets) that can result in accidents.

The three theories that I will cover can and have been used to model the causes and risks related to work accidents. Theories are not models of accident investigations, but models used to develop tools to investigate an accident. If you work in the field of industrial relations, you will want to know that the two dominant models are part of the functionalist paradigm and the lesser-known model, Dwyer's model, is part of the radical structuralism paradigm according to industrial relations nomenclature.

I address the problem of workplace accidents from different angles of paradigmatic research. I then study the methodologies and epistemology - a branch of philosophy that studies how we make science - that is characteristic for each theory. I explore the differences between the three models, as well as those between the three theories, and draw conclusions about their current and future uses. Finally, I demonstrate that the classical epidemiological models are incomplete and cannot alone explain all the actions and social structures that occur during a workplace accident. To try to uncover the truth, practitioners need to incorporate theories that are outside of functionalist models, such as Dwyer's, into their work. For complex investigations, we need to use systemic models that incorporate both the functionalist and radical structuralism paradigm. This runs counter to current thinking and practice, where the majority of investigators are married to the traditional way of finding *whodunit.*

DETERMINING DETERMINISM

Following the Second World War, we started to become interested in the way workers use information. Research gave rise to two distinct theoretical approaches in the industrial relations world: the first was linked to the tradition of the natural sciences and the second was related to cognitive science. We find ourselves in the realm of objectivism and determinism, where there is a proliferation of theories and the conception of mostly systemic theoretical models. Before going further, I want to provide my definitions of objectivity and determinism as related to investigative work.

We refer to concepts as being objective when they are true independently of our own perception, emotions, and imagination. Anti-objectivity or individual subjectivity is the opposite. We consider a theory or the conclusions of an investigation to be objectively true when the proposition(s) and condition(s) are determined without bias caused by a sentient subject (scientist or investigator). Scientific and investigation objectivity refers to the ability to judge without partiality or external influence.

When we determine something to be true, such as the causal and contributing factors leading to an accident, we may also be determining the prior conditions and natural laws that led to the occurrence. We call this determinism, the philosophical idea that all events, including moral choices, are determined by previously existing causes. When I use the term determinism in this book, I mean causal determinism that we know in physics as cause-and-effect. When I claim that there is no determinism, I mean that scientists cannot claim with absolute certainty that their theories are the absolute truth. When I mention that investigators cannot claim that they have identified the true causes of an accident, I am saying that there is no such thing as absolute certainty in investigation work.

I will be coming back to these two concepts, objectivity and subjectivity (anti-objectivity) quite often. I will also mention determinism and causal determinism at several points. I summarized these concepts so that you may understand that my main arguments are that there is no such thing as the truth and that the truth is in the eye of the beholder. The latter is an individual, a scientist, an investigator, and a community of people sharing the same beliefs. We can use objective or subjective observations and theories to reach conclusions about the failures we investigate. Regardless of the method and theory used, we can never claim that we know the absolute truth about the causes and contributory factors that lead to an accident. There is no such thing as being able to determine with absolute certainty why we fail and why failure occurred.

TOM DWYER'S FORGOTTEN THEORY

Dwyer is the first and one of the only researchers to have developed a theoretical framework that uses sociological factors to explain the rate of accidents at work. He supported his research using statistics (quantitative method) that allowed him to validate his hypothesis. Dwyer did not stop at a theory about occupational accidents, he sought and managed to explain how we could use a sociological approach to understand how to overcome a major problem that was prevalent in the 1970s and '80s, namely the lack of accident prevention. Dwyer developed an investigation model based on a sociological theory of accidents, stating:

> *Armed with a heterodox training … [including] training in business administration, symbolic interactionism, structuralist and Marxist anthropologies, organizational sociology, and theory building, I would carry out an ethnographic study on a New Zealand construction site …. This would provide initial insight … into what would become a sociological theory of industrial accidents* (Dwyer, 1991).

Dwyer postulates that it is necessary to analyze how management deals with the risk ratio for workers at three levels. First, he considers the use of rewards (reward level) in industry, such as compensating for overtime. Second, he researched the use of sanctions and forms of authority (command level) that may hinder or motivate workers.

Finally, he analyzes the risk that workers take according to their knowledge of the purpose of their work (organizational level). To interpret these sociological factors, Dwyer identified businesses that have day and night shifts in order to compare the different forms of social relationships in the same technology-based work environment. He therefore explains accident rates through social relations.

To understand Dwyer's theory, it is best to show the results of at least two of his monographs. I will take monographs Plant R and Factory P, as named by Dwyer, as examples. It is important to know that the factories Dwyer examined were operational in 1975 in France and New Zealand. Plant R has large vats where chemical reactions take place at very high temperatures. The product is highly volatile and any faults in production can result in serious damage to machinery. Factory P has large vats whose products are mixed at high temperatures. Under these conditions of production, the materials involved are very volatile and can be very dangerous even when they cool down. At first look, the processes are comparable in both plants. However, the social systems are different, which is a key component described in the model.

Dwyer compiled information from both factories under the three social levels I mentioned earlier. For Plant R he noted that, under the reward category, there were no financial incentives related to employee productivity. When workers would work overtime, fatigue ensued, causing carelessness. In fact, one in two accidents involved a worker on overtime. He noted, under the category he calls sanctions and forms of authority (command level), that there was excellent teamwork in Plant R. There was also solidarity among workers, a strong union, supervisors who were close to their employees and recognized that they worked better without supervision. According to the workers, the interventions of upper management caused confusion and led to contradictory directives that created problems. The boss is often in the way. Finally, under the category of knowledge of workers (organizational level), Dwyer noted that in Plant R training was seen as imperative to ensure production and safety. He also noted, there was a general impression among the workers that their safety was compromised over the higher imperative of productivity. Workers may refuse work that they deem unsafe, but generally, they do not refuse to work.

Dwyer compared day and night shift workers in Plant R and found that there was a higher accident rate during the day. Support personnel (e.g., electricians) are less likely to be present during the night shift. There are a reduced number of supervisors. Workers are more relaxed. Night workers were also more productive; there was less broken machinery, better communication between workers, and better coverage for workers in need of rest.

He conducted the same exercise with Factory P. Dwyer noted that, under the reward category, workers received financial incentives such as bonuses related to their productivity. The incentive created the habit for workers to hurry. However, there was no correlation between the workers accelerating their pace to complete work and taking risks. There were, in fact, few accidents and few overtime hours worked. He noted, under the category sanctions and forms of authority (command level), that workers complained of management providing contradictory instructions during shift changes. Workers mentioned that they operated under authoritarian-style supervision. Workers had little respect for their supervisors, did not form a well-integrated group, and worked under a form of trade unionism. Workers perceived working conditions as unsatisfactory and contributing to accidents. Finally, under the category of knowledge of workers (organizational level), Dwyer found that there was a very rudimentary skill level with many examples of accidents related to a lack of training. Workers were at risk given that they were using poorly adapted and poorly maintained equipment. Moreover, and disturbingly, explosions had happened because unclean materials had been placed in tanks.

For Factory P, Dwyer compared day and night shift workers and found a lower rate of accidents in the day shift. During the night, staff would wear less safety equipment and did not keep the factory floor as clean. There were almost no supervisors on the floor; hence, less supervision. The social relationships were completely different (and completely different from Plant R). There was a higher risk of replacement and workers took risks to ensure production.

Dwyer found that there was a different accident rate between Plant R and Factory P, as well as a different accident rate depending on the working conditions between the day and night shifts. We can also conclude that accident rates are heavily influenced by social factors within a factory. A key finding of Dwyer's work is that to understand workplace accidents, we need to analyze the state of societal relationships. Social relations can influence the safety environment and produce industrial accidents.

In this theory, there is a correlation between accident rates, the existence of a form of "class struggle" (Neo-Marxism), and the appropriation of the means of production. The term "struggle" is used in the context of values and the structure of the system that can expose the flaws leading to accidents. As we have just seen, social factors and the conflicts that arise in a workplace can be a source of risk. Dwyer's theory of occupational accidents with its three levels of control offers a unique perspective from which to understand beliefs and customs.

Dwyer's theoretical model allows the empirical verification of its assumptions using the development of an experimental scheme. He developed this model because of his interest in human nature and the relationship between the worker and his environment. His empirical research led him to a theory that he refined after the crash of the *Challenger* shuttle in 1986. He acknowledged that his theory was not definitive and universal. It is not an orthodox theoretical model; it is, in fact, on its own an untenable model to explain accidents. Put in another way in my own words, you can only uncover part of the truth if you use this radical structuralism investigation theory.

One of my conclusions from studying Dwyer's model is that to find out the truth, we need to examine the social relationships at play in a work environment. This is rarely, if ever, done when investigators and coroners look into accidents and disasters. In my eight years as lead of an investigation body, I have not found one example of an investigation team anywhere in the world that examined social factors in depth. This does not mean that the examination is not done and has not been done. I am saying, however, that exhaustively examining social factors is not a normal part of an investigation. We study human factors, but skim over the social factors. I will cover this a bit more in the next chapter.

UNDERPINNING INVESTIGATION THEORIES

Investigators traditionally base their investigation models on a few complex linear theories, the epidemiological theories. To properly trace the epistemology - the study of the nature of knowledge - of these theories, it is important to define what we mean when we refer to human factors in work-related accidents. Indeed, it is largely due to the work of human factors specialists that these theoretical models were developed.

The term human factor refers to people (workers) and their interactions with other people and their workplace (including equipment, working environment, working conditions, etc.). The study of human factors is very close to that of ergonomics, which got its name in 1949 from the Greek "ergon" (work) and "nomos" (natural law). We attribute the term to K.F.H. Murrell, after he hosted a meeting in London to discuss the role of humans in accomplishing work (Orlady, 1999).

The aeronautics industry is mainly credited for putting the term human factors into common use to solve practical problems in many spheres of the labour market. It is thanks to the work of Professor Elwyn Edwards and, later, of Frank Hawkins, that a practical model of human factors interpretation emerged, the SHELL model. An illustration of the model was published for the first time in a 1984 paper submitted by Frank Hawkins to the European Community (see Figure 2). Edwards defines human factors in his theory as follows: *"Human Factors is concerned to optimize the relationship between people and their activities, by the systematic application of the human sciences, integrated within the framework of systems engineering"* (Hawkins, 1987).

The traditional approach to accident prevention is focused on finding ways to reduce the risk of a recurrence of what is considered dangerous. We review the chronology of events or the circumstances that led a worker to carry out a dangerous act that caused an accident. Sometimes we realize that the same act may have been carried out hundreds of times before the accident without ever leading to unfortunate consequences. We may ask ourselves if the origin of the work accident is a random dangerous act. We can make many efforts to correct what we feel is the immediate cause of an accident without success. The same accident is repeated.

The SHELL model was developed by Elwyn Edwards in 1972 to explain the different interactions between workers and their environments. SHELL is an acronym for Software, Hardware, Environment, and Liveware. Within the acronym, "Liveware" refers to the system's human-human interactions, including such factors as management, supervision, crew interactions, and communications. "Hardware" refers to the equipment part of a transportation system or in an industry. It includes the design of workstations, displays, controls, seats, etc. "Software" refers to the non-physical part of the system including organizational policies, procedures, manuals, checklist layout, charts, maps, advisories, and increasingly, computer programs.

Finally, "Environment" includes the internal and external climate, temperature, visibility, vibration, noise, and other factors that constitute the conditions within which people are working. Sometimes the broad political and economic constraints under which the workplace system operates are included in this element. The regulatory climate is a part of the environment in as much as its climate affects communications, decision-making, control, and coordination.

The model helps to demonstrate that a workplace is an integral part of a complex work system. Workers are one component, along with other elements such as the equipment used by the workers, the tasks they carry out, and the environment in which these tasks are done.

Workplace accidents, according to this theory, occur in an open system. The model focuses on the worker (liveware) as the central element, identifying all of the human factors that affect worker performance. With this model, it is possible to identify all the elements of the system and identify the interactions between them.

The SHELL model covers not only the four components, but also the relationships - or interfaces - between the liveware and all the other components. *Figure 2* attempts to portray the fact that a match or mismatch of the interfaces is just as important as the characteristics of the blocks themselves. A mismatch can be a source of human error and the identification of a mismatch may be the identification of a safety deficiency in the system.

Edwards postulates that the elements themselves are just as important as the contacts between them. A bad match can be a source of error that leads to an accident at work. To understand the model, it is important to describe each element. The most valuable and flexible component in the system is the human element, the liveware, which is at the centre of the model. Each person brings his or her own capabilities and limitations, be they physical, physiological, psychological, or psychosocial. You can apply this component to any person involved with the operation or in support of the operation. The person under consideration interacts directly with each one of the four other elements. The person and each interaction, or interface (connections between elements), constitute potential areas of human performance investigation.

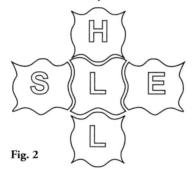

Fig. 2

There is another accident analysis model that is used by all experts in the field of occupational accidents to determine the chronology of the events that led to an accident and, by the same token, the causes and contributing factors to an accident. This is the theoretical model of James Reason, published in 1990. In his model, Reason emphasizes the importance of considering the latent factors that lead to workplace accidents. He recommends reviewing the many management and work methods established well before the accident, and trying to establish how these methods contributed to the accident.

Professor Reason is well acquainted with the work of Edwards and Hawkins. To develop his theory, he also used the work of Jens Rasmussen, a Danish professor who specialized in the field of occupational accidents. Reason's knowledge of cognitive psychology allowed him to develop his model after many disasters in the mid-1970s, including the nuclear accident at Three Mile Island. Today, developments in cognitive psychology have given the study of human errors a place of honour. We realize that the impacts of accidents at work can have regional or even international implications. The Chernobyl nuclear disaster affected an entire continent and plumes of nuclear dust likely travelled the globe. It was then that Reason began to theorize about workplace accidents. For Reason, it is important to be able to not only describe the desired manner of performing a job (what we saw in the first chapter), but also to be able to predict potential flaws.

In the Reason model, operators and work crews do not make mistakes with intent to harm (except in the case of sabotage). It sometimes happens that a safety device fails and that a workplace accident occurs despite the fact that the methods to produce the widgets are sophisticated and well thought through. Even if companies provide safety devices to detect and correct most human errors before an accident occurs, we must not forget to analyze this possible component of the work system.

A detailed *ex post facto* analysis of an occupational accident can shed light on situations and conditions that are prone to error. For example, one can discover situations that force the operator to act in such a way that he or she commits dangerous acts. This may be because the individual was not authorized to act, deviated from the standard practice, or misunderstood the act due to a communication problem within the workplace. Management decisions and company procedures can also have a tendency to create unsafe conditions in the workplace.

Reason's model is based on five elements that describe the same activity in the workplace from a different perspective, ranging from the situation closest to the time of the accident to measures or decisions that may have been made a long time prior to the accident. These latent and active failures are illustrated in Figure 3.

SWISS CHEESE MODEL

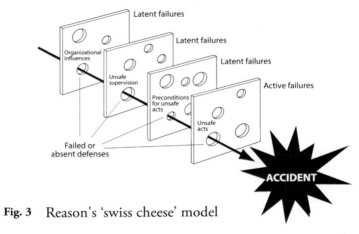

Fig. 3 Reason's 'swiss cheese' model

First, there are the decision-makers. These are the people that influence the way others work, the organizational influences. These people are responsible for the strategic management of available resources to achieve and balance the objectives of safety and efficiency. They include regulators, senior management, manufacturers, builders, and engineers.

Second, we have the line managers. These include all those who respond to management decisions by developing maintenance and operating procedures and by managing day-to-day activities. This includes people who set the hours of work for the day, develop the work team composition, oversee training, and supervise.

Thirdly, there are the preconditions for unsafe acts that flow from management decisions and management actions. This element looks at the steps taken to ensure that workers have equipment in good working order, a good knowledge of their work environment, a sufficient quantity of rest, low stress levels, good motivation, etc.

Fourthly, and fifthly, there are productive activities and defences, elements that immediately lead to unsafe acts. These are the active failures and include measures and decisions made during work that have a direct impact on worker safety. These also include safety devices, such as the different components put in place to prevent injuries, damage, and costly service interruptions in the event of a dangerous act. Safety devices are not only limited to physical protection devices, but also include rules, regulations, security measures, etc.

The Reason model is often referred to as "Swiss Cheese," for obvious reasons if you look at the model in *Figure 3*. The model also falls under the functionalist (objectivist) paradigm for those who work or study in the field of industrial relations. What is essential to understand in this theoretical model is that errors can occur in all elements, but an accident happens in the workplace only when errors in all of the elements align. During an investigation, we experiment to reproduce the scheme that led to the accident in order to make an empirical verification of our hypotheses.

Reason makes a distinction between active failures and latent conditions that lead to failures. An active failure is an error or violation that has an immediate negative effect on the safety of the work environment. Active failures are the circumstances or the situations that immediately precede and lead to the accident. A latent condition is the result of a decision or action taken before the accident; it can take time to manifest itself. Decision-makers, regulators, and management (i.e., people removed from the accident, both in space and time) can implement hazardous conditions. Examples of latent conditions include inadequate procedures and regulations, an overly demanding workload, a training problem, etc. These failures can be in place long before a workplace accident occurs. Everything takes place before the accident.

There is a risk of an accident when human actions interact with hazardous conditions in the immediate and external work environment. We use Reason's model to reconstruct workers' actions and determine the conditions that made these acts dangerous. You can easily do this yourself anytime you want to assess something that went wrong. I use this method to write detective novels. You go back as far as you can before the event you want to analyze: an accident, a murder, or even the argument you just had with a co-worker.

Investigators use Reason's model to produce a framework for developing an occurrence sequence. As well, the model facilitates the organization of data about the work system collected using the SHELL model, and improves our understanding of their influence on human performance. The occurrence sequence is developed by arranging the information regarding occurrence events and circumstances around one of five production elements: decision-makers, line management, preconditions, productive activities, and defences. If you want to use this framework to produce a post-mortem report of a failed endeavour, just mirror these five production elements with those that played a role in your own work environment. I will show you a practical method for how to reconstruct failure at the end of the next chapter, but here are some general guidelines on how investigators do their work.

We align the production elements in a chronological context - a sequence of events. This temporal aspect is an important organizing factor since the events and circumstances that can lead to an accident or incident are not necessarily proximate in time or in location to the site of occurrence. Investigators establish a sequential ordering of the data. This is, in Reason's terms, ordering of active and latent factors.

Active factors are the final events or circumstances that led to an occurrence. Their effect is often immediate because they occur either directly in the system defences (such as disabled warning systems) or at the site of the productive activities (such as a problem in the integrated activities of the work system's liveware, software, and hardware elements that would indirectly result in a breaching of the system's defences).

Underlying or latent unsafe conditions may reside at both the individual and the organizational levels, and they may be present in the conditions that exist within a given work system (referred to as the "preconditions" element in Reason's model). Examples of latent unsafe conditions include inadequate regulations, inadequate procedures, insufficient training, high workload, and undue time pressure.

Some investigation organizations take the Reason model a bit further. They use variants of the "Swiss Cheese" model of human error. One such system is the Human Factors Analysis and Classification System (HFACS) that identifies the human causes of an accident. This model defines 19 causal categories within the four levels of human failure (unsafe acts, preconditions of unsafe acts, unsafe supervision, and organizational influences). Dr. Scott Shappell and Dr. Doug Wiegmann from, respectively, the Civil Aviation Medical Institute and University of Illinois at Urbana-Champaign, USA, developed HFACS in response to a trend that showed some form of human error to be the primary causal factor in 80 percent of all flight accidents in the navy and marine corps.

THE AGE OF REASONING

John Rogers Commons, an institutional economist and labour historian (among other qualifications), once explained that there is no antagonism between a theory and a practice because a theory is only a tool for investigating practices, like a shovel used to dig for facts and convert them into an understandable system. As I compare and analyze accident causation theories, I will be looking at how we can use the various theories to develop systemic investigation models. As investigators, we need to understand why accidents happen, but our goal is to trace most of the elements that led to the accident and thus produce knowledge that can then serve, for example, to change laws, regulations, procedures, and practices. We need to understand the system at play. Theoretical models are useful to understand how accidents happen; they do not explain how an industrial environment functions.

Investigators construct investigation models. We empirically and objectively collect data that explains the causes and risks. We employ logical reasoning. We want to go further than a model that analyzes only technological or economic contexts. We need to use a model that relies mainly on causal determinism. In the end, our prime objective is to identify professional relationships and examine the multiple interactions within them. We use logical reasoning to reach logical conclusions. We can accomplish this by using deductive reasoning, abductive reasoning or, inductive reasoning.

When we deduct we put forward a consequence necessarily ensuing from previously established assumptions. A classic form of deduction is the syllogism, a perfected rhetorical figure linking a general statement, a middle term and a conclusion. For example, one type of syllogism would state "Iron may rust, this item is made of iron, this item may rust." Although they seldom deploy this classic figure in their work, investigators use its logical rules to determine consequences. In turn, new consequences become established assumptions or additional facts to use in other reasoning techniques.

When we use abductive reasoning, we test our hypotheses based on the best information that is available to us. We make an educated guess. We generally start with an incomplete set of observations that lead us to the most probable explanation. We often do this when there is no clear explanation to our observed phenomenon. For example, you briefly leave the kitchen to answer the phone in your study. You leave your baby daughter in her highchair eating her chocolate pudding. Your eldest son walks by you while you are on the phone and says he is going out, and exits through the kitchen door. As you return to the kitchen, the pudding is splattered all over the walls and floor. Your son is gone. You conclude your baby daughter made the mess on her own. It is a proper assumption, but it could be false. Your son could be responsible, but it is an unlikely conclusion. Abductive reasoning is not a good way to draw investigation conclusions, but it does help to form hypotheses that can be checked through inductive reasoning.

We attribute inductivism, or inductive reasoning, to Francis Bacon who was, among other things, a philosopher and scientist in the 17th century. In this model, one observes nature, proposes a modest law, and then confirms it by several observations. We discard laws that do not conform to our findings. Laws grow broader, never exceeding careful observation. We can then uncover nature's causal and material structure. When investigators use inductive reasoning, they proceed by using a large set of data or combining the findings of several investigations.

They use data to discern a pattern, they generalize, and then they infer a cause or contributing factor. For example, inductive logic helps us determine that seat belts save lives. Investigators collect data on accidents where occupants of the vehicles were either wearing or not wearing their seat belts. They can discern that, if the data shows a higher fatality rate for those not wearing safety belts, that seat belts save lives.

Investigators are constantly asking the question "Why?" Their answer follows the word "Because." An oversimplified example could be "Why did the driver die?" "Because he was not wearing his seat belt." Investigators fall easily into circular reasoning: "A is true because B is true; B is true because A is true." This is what the epidemiological theoretical models of occupational accidents (SHELL and Reason) teach them to do in order to understand complex contexts. This is a theoretical model strength but also a weakness as it leads to generalization as we identify causes and contributing factors for a particular situation instead of understanding the constraints and reasons behind the events. We can determine that seat belts save lives, but we may overlook why people do not wear seat belts.

When establishing a sequence of events, if investigators asked themselves the question "Why do people drive without seat belts?" they are stepping outside the causal and epidemiological theoretical models (functionalist models). Even though most investigators do not know this, they are using systemic theories. They would be studying social relations and not truncated facts that give rise to an episodic event. The study of social behaviour is much more difficult with functionalist (objectivist) models, such as Edwards's and Reason's models. Dwyer's theory is an example of how we can study social behaviour, although it is not a comprehensive model that can be qualified as a systemic theory. For Dwyer, social relations are central. As we have demonstrated above, Dwyer's sociological model also makes it possible to go beyond circular reasoning and look at the problem from a very different angle much more conducive to understanding the dynamic social interactions and vulnerabilities.

Although Dwyer's sociological model has never made it onto the radar of specialists in the field of occupational accidents, we somewhat use his theory - and investigation methodology - when looking into the sociological factors that lead to failure. In fact, if investigation bodies are lucky enough to have ergonomists or other human factors specialists, the investigation team will use methods and techniques more closely associated with scientific research, theoretical work that helps uncover what went wrong in the system. Social scientists, including human factors specialists, are often better equipped than technical practitioners to identify risks and establish model defences, since this is what they do to acquire their licence to practise and their focus when they conduct doctoral research. Human factors specialists study dynamic social interactions and vulnerabilities, the main topic of the next chapter.

PLANNED WORK, PERFORMANCE IN A NON-LINEAR FASHION

Work environments are complex and unpredictable; they are non-deterministic environments. Workers have complex behaviours. Workers do not conduct their work in a linear fashion. They do not conduct their activities as planned; they have patterns of activity to achieve a particular purpose in a particular work environment. There are many variables, shifting goals, and unpredictable demands. There is a difference between creating work environments and actually conducting the tasks. There is a difference between prescribed tasks and actual activities carried out at a work site. The jargon used to describe this discrepancy in the ergonomics and safety world is "work-as-imagined" and "work-as-done." The work-as-done differs from the work-as-imagined. The imagined work takes place within the limitations and anomalies of an actual environment. We cannot predict work-as-done. Ergonomists know this. Work-as-done may lead to accidents, as noted by Sidney Dekker, a professor and director in the Key Centre for Ethics, Law, Justice and Governance at Griffith University in Brisbane, Australia:

"(…) Accidents are preceded by normal, daily successful work. This will likely include so-called 'workarounds' and daily frustrations, the improvisations and adaptations, the shortcuts, as well as the sometimes

unworkable or unfindable tools, user-friendly technologies, computers that lock up, and occasionally unreliable results or readings from various instruments and measurements" (Dekker, 2016).

Workers may change their strategies and adapt to the variations that naturally occur in a work environment. Investigators do not spend much time, if any, comparing work-as-done with work-as-imagined. Investigators are comfortable identifying failures in the system using a linear approach, backtracking from the event to identify root causes. They are comfortable using circular reasoning. However, the work-as-done - the planned work - is not linear. Workers have practices and non-linear methods of carrying out tasks. Workers continuously adjust what they do, at times creating workarounds. A worker adapts and improvises solutions.

A complete investigation requires visualizing the full picture of failure. This includes capturing both the linear timeline of events and looking at the complex relationships that exist between all the relationships that aligned to produce an accident. We need to consider the variability in normal system performance. The premise is that failure can result from individuals and organizations adapting to their work environments in order to cope with the complexity of that environment. Accidents do not occur simply because of a breakdown or a malfunction; they can also occur because workers and organizations adjust their actions to meet changes in demand and resource needs. Performance varies according to unexpected functions that cause breakdowns or malfunctions. Individuals and organizations continually adjust their performance to match current conditions. Failure also happens because organizations, groups, and individuals do not properly anticipate the changing shape of risk. Investigators need to understand the performance conditions, which are not generally very specific - underspecified - at the work site.

Let me give you an oversimplified example. A gentleman farmer is pretty annoyed with the fox that keeps attacking his chickens. He grabs his shotgun and takes off after seeing the villain with one of his birds. Unbeknownst to him, his neighbour is out picking mushrooms nearby; he is wearing a proper orange identification vest but is bent over behind a tree rendering his back invisible. The farmer takes aim at the fox but misses his target and instead hits his neighbour, wounding him. We have all heard stories about a hunter discharging a firearm after having mistaken a human for the target. If you are investigating the accident and only have the usual training supplied to normal investigators, you look at all the factors that could have led to the mistake, including the target, time of day, training, experience, expertise, etc. You are investigating using the typical sequential and epidemiological models.

The mandatory training and regulatory requirements regarding methods and techniques to shoot at a target are very rudimentary. For example, the official Department of Justice Canada Handbook on firearms safety has a small insert regarding safety when shooting at a target: "Before shooting, be sure of the target." (!) "Can you clearly see the target?" (!) "Is there anything else that can suddenly appear in the line of fire?" The performance conditions are not clearly defined. You cannot identify all of the various conditions that a hunter may encounter that could affect performance (e.g., bad weather, camouflaged colours, distracting noises, silhouettes, emotional influences arising from adrenaline and rage at the fox, etc.). You are taught that you will encounter people walking in the woods, but you are not necessarily taught that you can encounter mushroom pickers, bent over. There is no material out there to explain how the farmer and neighbour conducted their work-as-done. There is some guidance on how work-is-done, such as the Department of Justice Handbook and some hunting manuals, but it is limited.

If you are using the Swiss Cheese model to investigate the hunting accident, you may identify the various interdependencies (the holes in the cheese that can grow or shrink), but you would not necessarily examine the full impact of these factors - how the normal performance varies and can combine dynamically to lead to an accident. Circular reasoning may help you make sense of some of the factors and may give you a degree of clarity, but you will have difficulties identifying performance.

You would identify the factor of a neighbour being in the way. You may not identify him bending over behind a tree and looking like a target. You may identify the various conditions, such as poor weather, but may not study the position of the sun in the sky and its potential to reflect on the scope of the rifle. You may not determine the full impact of all the facts: variations in the environment and the farmer's own performance that affected him while racing to get to the top of the hill, out of breath and pumped up. Generally, investigators stick to what happened and do not examine the large-scale factors - sociological, economic, and political considerations - that lead to accidents.

If you want to find the underlying cause of the accident and uncover all of the contributing factors, you need to investigate the practices, not just the actions. You need to identify and assess the performance conditions. You do this by replacing the actions with practices. To help with this, investigators need to identify patterns and functional interdependencies. They need to understand messy details, like the practices of the hunters and the mushroom gatherers - the practice of the workers.

From there, investigators can begin to identify safety procedures, key safety messages, and potential training requirements. If we want to learn about principles behind hunting and develop tools to help visualize the environmental conditions, you need to analyze how the performance failed. Then, it is possible to explain the complexity of hunting and identify potential sources of incidents. Investigating for performance requires studying the interaction of the environment with various components, subsystems, software, organizations, human behaviours, and human practices. You need to study the work-as-done, not just the way work-is-imagined. This requires a long and detailed human factors (social) study. It may also require economical and political analysis. This is not what investigators normally do. Investigators come up with true causes and contributing factors, but they do not always come up with the truth that can improve safety.

PUTTING THEORIES INTO PRACTICE

The SHELL model and James Reason's models use the notion that the worker is part of an open system. The environment influences all parties, including the outputs, inputs, and activities of workers. The approach of these models allows us to study the phenomenon of feedback, reactions from the actions. Workers adjust to feedback automatically or voluntarily. Feedback causes them to modify their actions that can lead to accidents.

Investigators spend most of their time concerned with the static and descriptive aspect of the elements and little on the dynamic aspect (the relationships between variables, the notions of power, conflict, and change, both at the level of the organization and in society, the informal aspects of internal and external relations to the organization). The present tools used by investigators suffer from low predictive ability. Investigators generally reconstruct parts of an accident by taking into account that the events occur in an orderly system. They are generally silent about the social interaction between actors in the system. Essentially, investigators understand the actors as interacting harmoniously, as if there is a consensus between them on the values and structures of the system. They do not look deeper to see if there is a struggle between them. Simple and complex linear theories do not properly set up the investigator to study the social or organizational system, a significant part of the environment that can lead to an unbalanced or dangerously influenced system.

To understand what caused an accident and the risk factors that exist in the workplace, the theoretical models must examine the impacts of the external and internal environments while understanding the interactions of a work structure with its effects and its results. The frame of reference must involve the three actors of the workplace (employees, employers, and governments). While the epidemiological theories include all the actors, radical structuralism models may not. Dwyer's model, for example, excludes governments, which have their own objectives, values, and powers. It is unrealistic to think that the state remains a neutral arbiter while it has its own interests. A complete theory must include an analysis of rules, contexts, and the whole body of governmental ideas and ideologies.

We have traced the epistemology of the three theories. Dwyer's model is mainly a neo-Marxist view of the world. The SHELL and the Swiss Cheese models align with the realm of ergonomics and cognitive psychology. Experts in the field of investigations must understand that they need to use theories with different epistemology roots if they want to explain what caused an accident and identify all risk factors. Further, they should understand that investigations require the involvement of many specialists in the technical and human factors fields.

Our traditional investigation practices have allowed us to pick the low-hanging fruit. It was relatively new a few decades ago to come up with conclusions such as "seat belts save lives." Today, investigation reports are often redundant. The level of effort required to move the safety yardstick further than the *status quo* is tremendous, since the functionalist theoretical models seem to have reached their limits.

Let me give a concrete example of an international challenge to safety that traditional investigation methods have not been able to eradicate. In all countries of the world, professional fish harvesting is either the most dangerous or one of the top three most dangerous professions, along with mining, policing, and firefighting. I will use this challenge - improving fish harvesters' safety - to demonstrate the limitations of the SHELL and Swiss Cheese models and the benefits of a model like Dwyer's.

When we use epidemiological models that involve circular reasoning, we conclude there are a dozen factors that lead to accidents on professional fishing vessels (vessel instability, poor safety equipment, poor training, inappropriate labour standards, etc.). We are also able to determine that, most of the time, these twelve factors are interconnected. We stop our analysis at these factors, even if we know that the root of the problem may be economic, political, or social. There is often an analysis of the problem and we can conclude that fish harvesters accept that their work is dangerous and that risks are part of the job. As noted by Geoffrey W. Gill, in his book titled *Maritime Error Management,* *"The marine world still tends to be characterized by 'macho' can-do attitudes, and the belief that accidents are inevitable and simply part of getting the job done; act now - risk assess later"* (Gill, 2011). If you want to improve safety in fish harvesting, you must first understand why this culture still prevails. This is harder to do with circular models, since we may only narrow down our finding to a societal paradigm, without digging deeper down.

The addition of an anti-objectivist (subjectivity) theory in the practitioners' toolbox is essential if we want to do a comprehensive analysis of occupational accidents. We cannot understand work-related accidents by using only theoretical models based on the functionalist (objectivity) paradigm. It is preferable to explore causes and risks of accidents with models that also allow analysis of other social and philosophical issues in the workplace, such as conflict. In fact, at a minimum, it would be beneficial for health and safety investigators, inspectors, and coroners to combine approaches. It is therefore worthwhile for practitioners to look more closely at all theories in order to try to develop an investigation plan based on several methods, since they need to comprehensively understand all the risks in an organization or system that can lead to a workplace accident.

A more simplified way of looking at accident theories is to say that there are theories that fall into a more objective way of describing the work, a functionalist theory. When we can say that there is a blind spot when you turn into a street, potentially leading to an accident, you are providing an objective assessment. Then there are theories that fall into a more subjective way of describing work, a radical structuralism theory. When we say that we believe that stress or fatigue may lead to a driver missing the turn, you are providing a subjective assessment.

We need to look at accidents both in an objective and subjective way. We also need to dig deeper. Naming the safety issue is not sufficient. Take the above-mentioned example of culture in fish harvesting. It is already an advancement to find a behavioural problem, but accidents will continue to happen unless we can qualify why workers have practices that lead to the way work-is-done.

The SHELL and Swiss Cheese models do not study the forces that generate conflict - a cultural conflict, for example. For that reason, these models are not well suited to identify the danger posed by the culture of risk that exists among professional fish harvesters. To draw the conclusion that a systemic social problem exists, practitioners who limit themselves to these two theories must study dozens of similar cases, if not hundreds. A single accident is not enough to detect a systemic social problem. Hawkins and Reason developed their models to analyze a single accident and not to draw a conclusion following many similar accidents.

In Dwyer's model, we try to understand the power struggle, the conflict between actors who do not share the same values. In Dwyer's model, unlike the SHELL and Swiss Cheese models, the foundation of the approach focuses on an imbalance of power between employers and workers in all respects. There is dominance of one over the other (e.g., supervision of an authoritarian style and contradictory guidelines). There are issues of power and domination in any economic and technological system, with each group defining their own interpretation of efficiency. Dwyer studies the result of the conflict between classes (management and employees). According to Dwyer, accidents are the result of the alienation of workers from a social class.

The three models look at the actors and the way the processes they generate affect them. Only Dwyer's model considers the context; he draws conclusions based on quantitative data (comparisons between different plant rates) and a comparative social analysis. On the other hand, a major weakness of Dwyer's model is that it does not capture all of the spatiotemporal data that is part of the work environment. It is a little more subjective, even if the three theories are objective. Indeed, even if less developed in Dwyer's model, his theory measures sociological, psychological, and socioeconomic variables that are measurable and observable, and therefore objective.

CLOSING ARGUMENTS

Research continues on theoretical models of workplace accidents, most centred on measuring employee performance. Some authors analyze adaptation strategies, improvisations, negotiations, conflicts, and compromises put in place in order to repair hazards and obtain optimum safe results in the workplace. Many authors analyze, among other things, how workers adapt or negotiate their individual and collective action.

Investigators and workers' compensation professionals can measure the extent of certain problems and target certain causes or risks, but quantitative research is not enough. We know that the social world, including the work environments, is relative, but investigators spend little time understanding it. It is important to include in our methodology qualitative (ideographic) analyses. In order to understand what failed in the system, we must use different paradigmatic theoretical models to comprehensively understand occupational accidents.

The determinism of environmental forces in the life of organizations - and the identification of causes and risks related to accidents - has made immense progress in recent decades, mainly because of the work conducted by Perrow, Rasmussen, Reason, et al. Their work remains essential, but it cannot alone explain the margin of discretion that actors have to make choices that guide their action. Investigators need models that take into account voluntarism. It is therefore necessary to find and use methods that look into the left of the axis of the nature of the social sciences (towards subjectivism). Researchers need to spend time creating theoretical models that are influenced by subjectivism. An alternative to creating more theoretical models is to hand off the study of social behaviour to specialists in this field.

Social structures involved in a workplace accident are bipolar: objective and subjective. Practitioners would therefore benefit from using theories and practices to interpret the dual relationship of actions and social structures they examine. Practitioners would benefit from recognizing the limits to their simple linear and complex linear models and seeking help from experts in the various human factors field, including experts in social sciences.

III

Socially Induced Errors
Telling the Accident Story

> › *Team dynamic and training*
> › *Cultural differences in the workplace*
> › *Gynocentric and traditional perspectives*
> › *Uncovering the human factors behind accidents*
> › *Non-events are not non-factors*

I n March 1977, a separatist group exploded a bomb at Gran Canaria International Airport, forcing Spanish civil aviation authorities to divert incoming flights to nearby Los Rodeos, a regional airport, to wait out the danger.

It wouldn't take long for planes to crowd the smaller airport, now known as Tenerife North, which had only one runway, a main taxiway running parallel, and four shorter taxiways connecting the two. High-density cloud had formed, normal for Los Rodeos, which sits at 633 metres (2,077 feet) above sea level and where visibility varies wildly especially due to fog. One minute clear skies, the next *sopa de guisantes* (pea soup).

After the threat at Gran Canaria had been contained, authorities reopened the airport and flights were permitted to depart Los Rodeos. Given its configuration, and the gridlock on the ground, planes would need to taxi along Runway 30 to position for takeoff, a procedure known as a backtaxi or backtrack. This included two Boeing 747s, one from KLM and another from Pan Am.

The pilot of Pan Am 1736 wasn't happy. If the day's events weren't difficult enough, his plane's access to the runway had been blocked by a refueller topping up the fellow Jumbo. Turning to his co-pilot he spat, *"Dang Tenerife!"* He had no choice. With insufficient clearance to safely manoeuvre around the wide body, there was nothing to do but sit and watch smaller planes slip past - and the fog roll in.

Once KLM 4805 had completed fuelling, the air traffic controller radioed the cockpit. His English was good, but he had a clear accent and there was some nervousness in his voice. He instructed the pilot to backtaxi down the runway and make a 180-degree turn to get into takeoff position. The pilot acknowledged and the plane began to roll. The air traffic controller then instructed, *"Please report when ready for clearance."* The pilot and co-pilot were busy completing their checklist and would copy this clearance only after the aircraft was in takeoff position.

The air traffic controller then radioed the Pan Am crew to follow the KLM plane down the runway, to use the short taxiway at the third exit on the left, and continue along the main taxiway running parallel to the runway. Initially, both the pilot and co-pilot were unclear as to whether the controller had said first or third exit, so the pilot asked for clarification. The air traffic controller was emphatic: *"The third one, sir; one, two, three; third, third one."* The situation had become a bit tense.

As the Pan Am plane rolled along, the pilots identified the unmarked taxiways using an airport diagram. They identified the first two (C-1 and C-2), but not the third (C-3). There were no markings or signs for the exits and the poor visibility wasn't helping. They were unsure of their aircraft's position on the runway and also unaware that their taxiing instructions were flawed to begin with. (Accessing the third taxiway would have required a 148-degree turn that led back to the still-crowded main apron, and another 148-degree turn to continue toward the runway. It was like following an inverted "Z," a practical impossibility.)

Fog had now reduced visibility to less than 100 metres (330 feet).

Meanwhile, the KLM plane had reached the start of the runway where the pilot performed the 180-degree turn to ready for takeoff. Fog was forming 900 metres (3,000 feet) down the runway and moving toward the aircraft at approximately 12 knots (22 kilometres per hour), but, for the moment, the skies around them were clear.

Immediately after lining up, the pilot advanced the throttles and the aircraft started forward. The air traffic controller, partly distracted by a football (soccer) match on the radio in the tower, instructed the pilot on the route to follow after takeoff. His instructions included the word *"takeoff,"* but did not include an explicit statement that the aircraft was in fact cleared for takeoff. The co-pilot read the flight clearance back to the controller: *"We are now at takeoff."* The pilot interrupted, *"We're going."*

The air traffic controller, who could not see the runway due to the increased fog, initially responded with *"OK,"* non-standard terminology in air traffic control operations. This only reinforced the pilot's understanding that they had takeoff clearance. The air traffic controller misinterpreted and thought that the KLM plane was waiting in takeoff position. He added, *"Stand by for takeoff, I will call you,"* indicating that he had not intended to give takeoff clearance.

A simultaneous radio call from the Pan Am pilot caused interference on the radio frequency, which was audible in the KLM cockpit as a three-second-long shrill. This caused the KLM pilots to miss the crucial latter portion of the air traffic controller's response. The Pan Am's transmission was, *"We're still taxiing down the runway, the Clipper 1736!"* (referring to his plane's name and flight number). This message was also blocked by interference and inaudible to the KLM crew. If either message had been heard in the KLM cockpit, the crew might have aborted the takeoff.

Due to the fog, neither crew was able to see the other plane on the runway ahead of them-now on a collision course -nor could either aircraft be seen from the control tower. The fact that the airport was not equipped with ground radar made the situation even more dire.

It was only after the KLM plane had begun to roll that the air traffic controller instructed the Pan Am crew to *"Report when runway clear."* Pan Am's pilot replied, *"OK, will report when we're clear."* On hearing this, flight engineer aboard the KLM plane expressed concern that the Pan Am was indeed not clear of the runway, asking his two pilots, *"Is he not clear, that Pan American?"* The pilot emphatically replied, *"Oh, yes,"* and continued with the takeoff.

According to the cockpit voice recorder (CVR), the Pan Am co-pilot had said, *"There he is!"* when he spotted the landing lights of KLM 4805 through the fog as his plane neared the taxiway exit. When it became clear that the KLM aircraft was approaching at takeoff speed, Pan Am's pilot exclaimed, *"Goddamn, that son-of-a-bitch is coming,"* while the co-pilot yelled, *"Get off! Get off! Get off!"* The pilot applied full power to the throttles and made a sharp left turn toward the grass infield in an attempt to avoid the impending collision. It was too late. By the time the KLM pilots saw the Pan Am aircraft, they were already travelling too fast (300 kilometres an hour). In desperation, the pilot prematurely attempted a takeoff to clear the Pan Am plane, resulting in a severe tail strike.

The disaster remains the deadliest in aviation history. Miraculously, 61 survivors escaped the Pan Am wreckage, walking out onto the intact left wing through holes in the fuselage, the side away from the collision. Everyone aboard the KLM flight was killed.

The facts showed that there had been misinterpretations and false assumptions that led to the accident. Analysis of the CVR transcript showed that the KLM pilot was convinced that he had been cleared for takeoff, while the air traffic controller was certain that the flight 4805 was stationary at the end of the runway and awaiting takeoff clearance. The KLM co-pilot was not as certain about takeoff clearance as was his pilot. In particular, a Dutch investigation pointed out that the crowded airport had placed additional pressure on all parties, including the KLM cockpit crew, the Pan Am cockpit crew, and the controller.

This was one of the first accident investigations where investigators studied the influence of human factors. The resulting investigation led to sweeping changes to international airline regulations and aircraft procedures. Aviation authorities introduced requirements for standard phrases and a greater emphasis on English as a common working language. I will return to this last point later, when I talk about cultural differences.

Air traffic instructions should not be acknowledged solely by a colloquial phrase such as "OK," or even "Roger," (which simply means in official transport communications that the last transmission was received), but with a readback of the key parts of the instruction to show mutual understanding. This has been standard for bridge crews on ships long before the air mode decided to adopt this communication standard. The phrase "takeoff" is now used only when the actual takeoff clearance is given or when cancelling that same clearance (i.e., "Cleared for takeoff" or "Cancel takeoff clearance"). Additionally, an air traffic controller clearance given to an aircraft already lined up on the runway must be prefixed with the instruction "Hold position." Up until that point, aircrew and controllers used the word "departure" in their communication. For example, they would say, "Ready for departure."

Further, cockpit procedures were also changed. Hierarchical relations among crew members were flattened. More emphasis was placed on team decisions, with the team needing to reach mutual agreement. Less experienced flight crew members were encouraged to challenge their captains when they believed something was not correct, and captains were instructed to listen to their crew and evaluate all decisions in light of crew concerns. This concept was later expanded into what is known today as crew resource management (CRM), or bridge resource management (BRM) in the marine mode. Training in CRM or BRM is now mandatory for all airline pilots and masters of large vessels, respectively.

We can learn so much from understanding our behaviours as they relate to our social environments when we were young, including the differences in the ways boys and girls are educated. In this chapter, I narrow my exploration to learned social behaviour as it links to the development of errors. I explain discoveries about interactions between workers of various backgrounds, focusing on management errors under the purview of group dynamics.

* * *

THE INVESTIGATOR'S MAZE

In the previous mazes, I covered what might be on your mind before you deploy to an accident site and what questions could be on your mind as you organize the data you collected. This helped set the scene for the science that was covered in both chapters and could help you build the factual section and start your analysis. In this chapter we will cover theory to help you further develop the analysis section and come up with findings.

When the investigation team gets together and sketches out a first draft of the sequence of events that lead to an accident (we cover how to do this at the end of this chapter), they can start digging into socially induced errors. If I was investigating this airline disaster, I could come up with the following questions that would help me identify the material I would use to complete the sequence of events and finish the investigation, including completing a draft report.

· Did the Pan Am crew engage according to their cultural upbringing?

· Was the KLM pilot overconfident?

· How many ambiguous communications can you count?

· What language would everyone be comfortable using in an emergency?

· How many operational teams were trying to work together?

* * *

WORKING AS A TEAM

The idea of developing training to facilitate team dynamics originated from assessing the conclusions of similar accident reports, including this investigation. Investigators did not propose new training; they determined that there was an issue with the team. They performed an epidemiological investigation. Scientists and practitioners examined how human factors contributed to airline disasters and determined how humans interact in an operational environment. For the first time, scientists and practitioners found a common thread and determined that crew interact differently in operational environments according to how they are raised, both culturally and socially. The conclusions drawn are irrefutable: poor teamwork skills induced by culture and social upbringing can lead to mistakes.

There has now been extensive study on how human beings interact, communicate, and make decisions, regardless of the operational environment in which they are working. We have been able, in the past decades, to determine that humans react differently in operation settings and in work environments according to our upbringing; in fact, it is possible to identify similarities according to our cultures. Some scientific studies and investigations have also concluded that we react differently according to our gender. It is important to note that these findings are generalizations. Academics or specialists in the various fields are in no way pitting one characteristic against another to judge if there is a better way, a better culture, a better gender.

We all have values and beliefs that are engrained and are influenced by our cultural background. In some cultures, it is less common for individuals to question authority. This cultural characteristic emerged as a factor in the accident investigation involving Japan Airline Flight 2, which was flying from Tokyo to San Francisco on November 22, 1968. The pilot mistakenly landed the plane in shallow water, two and a half miles short of the runway. There was heavy fog at the time, but it was determined that the co-pilot had information to indicate an impending accident, but never alerted the pilot; had he challenged his superior, the accident might have been prevented. Fortunately, nobody was injured. Cultural differences and tendencies can become more pronounced when we experience adverse operational conditions, including emergencies. We quickly revert to our engrained beliefs and values.

Contrary to popular belief, lack of competence is not a common reason for accidents. In past decades, we have spent a great deal of time trying to understand how human beings interact, communicate, and make decisions in operational settings such as in hospitals, power plants, and aircraft cockpits. The team setting, and reactions within that team context, especially in times of intense activity and stress, is a common reason for accidents.

Examples of errors within teams include such things as preoccupation with minor technical problems, failure to delegate tasks and assign responsibilities, inadequate monitoring, failure to set priorities, failure to use data, failure to communicate intent and plans, and failure to detect and challenge deviations from standard operating procedures.

Successful teams emulate several common behaviours in critical situations. First, they have good situational awareness. Second, they obtain relevant information prior to difficult decision-making. Third, they are cautious, use safe strategies, and keep their options open for as long as possible. Fourth, a fundamental and very critical point, is that they build a shared mental model of the situation that allows them to make realistic decisions based on constraints. Finally, they work as a team. This means they share the workload and monitor progress by cross-checking each other.

Teams nowadays increasingly comprise employees from differing cultural backgrounds. Interaction between teams may even be in different operational languages. For example, English is the common language for air and marine transportation, but the majority of professionals in these industries use another language at home. Now think about how hard it is to learn a second language and have to communicate in it during a very tense situation. Communication failures, both verbal and non-verbal, can lead to catastrophic team failures.

The job of an investigator involves uncovering if the team worked well together or not. It is also about understanding the composition of the team, the predetermined mindsets of the team members, and the culture of the individuals in the team. In a workplace, an individual acts and evolves as a member of a team. Every work environment is part of a larger system or systems with multiple teams interacting.

To understand all possible sources of error, investigators must explore all facets of the human - the liveware. By placing the human at the centre of this research, we can identify how different relationships influence the decision-making of the individual and the team. We are able to determine where the work-as-imagined failed. We can do this using an epidemiological model, such as the SHELL theory *(see Chapter II)*, where the liveware is at the centre, but we succeed in investigation work only if we identify the characteristics and the performance of the individual. This is something that we mainly do if we apply a systemic model. Our search for the truth - a truism - must reflect how the individual came to commit an error. The science of error, just like all sciences, must rest its purpose on the human. Forget this fact, this purpose, and the investigator or the researcher can easily become lost.

To improve safety, you need to show stakeholders that you understand how humans commit errors. You need to demonstrate how a team commits errors. Simply put, the system or organization fails because people fail. Humans develop systems and structure organizations. Only humans can change and change the systems and the culture of an organization.

Today, most modern large workplaces manage safety by implementing a comprehensive safety system. In professional terms, we refer to a *bona fide* system as a safety management system (SMS) that includes the five basic elements promoted by the International Labor Organization: organizing, planning, implementation, evaluation, and action for improvement *(ILO, 2009)*.

You use an SMS to manage significant safety risks if you work for a large airline, a petroleum or chemical industry, or an electricity generation plant, to name a few examples. An SMS provides a systematic way to identify hazards and control risks. It is a business approach to safety. The system should set goals, and then plan and measure safety performance. An SMS needs to become part of the company culture and the team culture: *"The cornerstone of good safety management is commitment from the top. In matters of safety and pollution prevention it is the commitment, competence, attitudes and motivation of individuals at all levels that determine the end result"* (IMO, 1993). Investigators must examine the SMS, understanding that, at times, there may well be a strong safety culture within a company, but it may not be sufficiently robust to prevent poor performance.

BRINGING OUR CULTURE TO THE WORKPLACE

Professor Geert Hofstede, an anthropologist, is a pioneer and specialist in understanding how interpretative skills can help solve problems and provide the foundation for strong thinking and understanding work environments. Hofstede developed a framework for understanding the cultural differences between one country and another, one culture and another. I read his theory for the first time in 1997, when I devoured the book *Culture's Conse-quences: International Differences in Work-Related Values*, which was written in 1984. I was and remain fascinated by our cultural dimension, a hidden dimension that is necessary to describe human behaviour in a workplace, such as that taking place on the bridge of a ship, where several people from different cultural backgrounds may interact.

Hofstede was born in the Netherlands in 1928 and died in 2020. Like all of us, his early life experiences influenced his interests. In Hofstede's case, he developed a keen interest in the cultures of different countries, and in particular, the systems of values and practices that distinguish each country. He started realizing differ-ences in cultures when Germany invaded his country during the Second World War. He also observed other cultures during his visits to Indonesia and England. His experiences with cultural differences became deep seated; they influenced how he would identify various measurable and comparable dimensions between cultures. He studied engineering and eventually earned a doctorate in social psychology. Combining these two fields helped him develop his findings. Besides his studies, his practical experience was also instrumental in providing insight into the framework that he would conceive.

Hofstede worked as a psychologist and researcher for IBM, a large multinational with branches in over 70 countries that conducts business in at least 20 languages. This helped Hofstede gain practical managerial and industrial experience. He wanted to understand the cultural differences among company employees and determined that it was necessary to study the cultures of their different countries. He directed a large multinational survey between 1967 and 1973. He collected empirical data -information verifiable by observation -from IBM employees. The goal was to gather information to study national values across many countries.

He identified "dimensions" of national cultures. This conceptual framework allows researchers and investigators to use a metric to measure cultural differences between countries through the identification of polar opposites, such as good and bad, or high and low. However, I do want to emphasize there is no such thing as a bad or good culture. The work conducted allowed for the definition of desirable conditions or states of being that a national culture prefers. National cultures may value similar things, but to different extents and in different ways. Preferences exist in every country and these preferences are at the root of each culture. Hofstede claimed, *"The survival of mankind will depend to a large extent on the ability of people who think differently to act together"* (Hofstede, 2001).

The professor also studied organizational cultures. Every society has values, practises rituals, has heroes and symbols (objects or gestures that have meanings relating to its core values); they may all change over time, while our values do not. We acquire values at a young age from our parents, other family members, and friends. Our educational systems and structures help foster those values through life. We acquire values from our predecessors and pass those values to our own children. While practices can change over time, national dimensions are rooted in the innermost layer of culture (values). Values are the fundamental thoughts and beliefs of a society and are less likely to change.

Hofstede found four dimensions. The first is power distance, which refers to inequalities within a society. The second is uncertainty avoidance, which refers to a society's level of comfort with the unknown. The third is the opposition of individualism and collectivism, referring to the level of independence of societal members. The fourth is the opposition of masculinity and femininity; these are, as you may have guessed, characteristics associated with gender.

In 1991, social scientist Michael Harris Bond and his colleagues conducted a study of students in 23 countries using a survey instrument developed with Chinese employees and managers. Hofstede eventually collaborated with Bond, and they revealed a fifth dimension of culture, the opposition of long-term and short-term orientation (initially called Confucian dynamism). In 2010, Michael Minkov used the scores for this dimension and the World Values Survey *(see Notes at the end of this book)* to extend the scores to 93 countries. This led Geert Hofstede to identify a sixth and last dimension: indulgence versus restraint.

Hofstede measures dimensions in terms of poles, such as high power distance/low power distance. Using the results of the survey data, he placed countries somewhere between those poles based on the values they hold. I based or extracted the following explanation of the six dimensions from an article written by him *(Hofstede, 2011)*.

The first dimension, the power distance index, can be defined as *"the extent to which the less powerful members of organizations and institutions (like the family) accept and expect that power is distributed unequally."* In this dimension, individuals perceive inequality and equate lesser power with the followers, or the lower level. A country that scores high on the index signifies that hierarchy is clearly established and executed in society, without being doubted or questioned. A low score on the index signifies that people question authority and attempt to distribute power.

The second dimension is individualism versus collectivism. This index explores the *"degree to which people in a society are integrated into groups."* Individualistic societies have loose ties; often individuals relate more to their immediate family. They emphasize the "I" as opposed to the "we." Collective societies have more tightly integrated relationships; groups are often the extension of the family. These in-groups are loyal and support each other when a conflict arises with another in-group.

The third dimension is uncertainty avoidance index, defined as *"a society's tolerance for ambiguity,"* in which people embrace or avoid events that are unexpected, unknown, or out of the status quo. Societies that score high on this index opt for stiff codes of behaviour, guidelines, laws, and generally rely on absolute truth, or the belief that one lone truth dictates everything and people know what it is. A low score on this index shows more acceptance of differing thoughts or ideas. Society tends to impose fewer regulations, individuals are more accustomed to ambiguity, and the environment is less restrained and formal.

The fourth dimension is masculinity versus femininity. Hofstede defines masculinity as *"a preference in society for achievement, heroism, assertiveness, and material rewards for success."* Femininity represents *"a preference for cooperation, modesty, caring for the weak, and quality of life."* Women in the respective societies studied tend to display different values. In feminine societies, they share modest and caring views equally with men. Women are somewhat assertive and competitive in societies that are more masculine, but notably less so than men. In other words, they still recognize a gap between male and female values.

The fifth dimension is long-term orientation versus short-term orientation. This dimension associates a society's connection to the past with present and future actions/challenges. This is how we look at the present or into the future. When a society scores highly on the index for short-term degree, we tend to hold stronger ties to traditions. Steadfastness is valued. When a society scores highly on the index for long-term degree, we tend to view adaptation and circumstantial, pragmatic problem solving as a necessity.

The sixth and last dimension is indulgence versus restraint, a measure of happiness. We can summarize it as whether or not simple joys fulfill us. When a society is indulgent, it *"allows relatively free gratification of basic and natural human desires related to enjoying life and having fun."* When a society scores highly on the index related to restraint, it *"controls gratification of needs and regulates it by means of strict social norms."* Individuals in indulgent societies tend to believe themselves to be in control of their own lives and emotions. Restrained societies, on the other hand, believe other factors dictate their lives and emotions.

Putting together national scores (from 1 for the lowest to 100 for the highest), Hofstede's six-dimension model allows for an international comparison between cultures in different countries; he called this comparative research. Investigators use several dimensions to examine the behaviour of individuals and teams in times of normal operations and in times of stress. We know, for example, that the power distance index shows very high scores for Latin, Asian, and Arab countries and for certain African countries. On the other hand, Anglo and Germanic countries have a lower power distance (only 11 for Austria and 18 for Denmark). The United States has a 40, which is in the middle of the scale when compared to Guatemala, where the power distance is very high (95), and Israel, where it is very low (13).

Western societies are now multicultural. The workforce in industries comprises many immigrants and first-generation citizens brought up in the traditional and cultural values of another homeland. Truth differs from one culture to another. In collective cultures, individuals tend to accept their unequal status and show deference to leaders. This may affect their willingness to question decisions or actions. This is valuable information, for example, when we want to understand why a co-pilot did not intervene to correct an evident mistake by a pilot.

If you come from a traditional American, Canadian, or European family, your view of hierarchy differs from that of someone from South America or Asia. Both views are equally valid. If you fail to intervene because you see your senior colleague making what you think is a mistake, you may not be failing according to your cultural bias. You are expecting the boss, captain, or surgeon to be in command, as the custodian of knowledge and having the appropriate skills. The individual in command knows the truth and it is not your job to question their truth. Shifting this mindset around is not easy. Intervening is not how you were raised. In the same way, if you are in charge and avoid asking your team to double-check your actions, you may not be making a mistake according to your cultural bias. Changing your behaviour may also be a very difficult task. When there is failure because of poor teamwork, we cannot blame the culture. We may find, instead, that there was a lack of understanding around cultural differences.

Cultures, Hofstede might have said, are at different poles of the power distance spectrum.

Investigators study performance and attitudes, but rarely do they study personalities. They do not dig into most human dimensions very frequently, if ever. You may, nevertheless, be intrigued to discover how some societies differ. There is much to learn about how societies behave, how we are wired together, and the cultural biases we bring to the workplace. I will give you a few examples.

Hofstede's fourth dimension, masculinity, is extremely low in Nordic countries, where Norway scores 8 and Sweden only 5. In contrast, masculinity is very high in Japan, which scores 95, and in countries influenced by German culture, such as Hungary, Austria, and Switzerland. In countries that speak English or have been influenced by the United Kingdom, masculinity scores are relatively high at 66. Interestingly, Latin countries present contrasting scores, where Venezuela has a score of 73, whereas Chile has a score of only 28. Germany scores high in uncertainty avoidance at 65 and Belgium even more at 94, compared to Sweden at 29 or Denmark at 23, despite their geographic proximity. However, few countries score very low in uncertainty avoidance.

Investigators can use these observations to identify how an organization is managed and how workers interacted with each other long before, immediately before, and even after an accident (during the emergency response, for example). In today's world with multicultural work teams, it becomes important to look at the role of culture and determine how the team will or should work together.

People of different nationalities not only differ in their response to authority, but also on how they deal with uncertainty and ambiguity. We all have our own ways of expressing our individuality. We are not all attuned in the same way to the collective needs of the group (the team or the industry organization). The motivating forces that can lead people to erroneous behaviours can derive from an individual's culture or from the culture of the organization, a powerful ingredient that can lead to calamitous results. The disastrous explosion in 1986 at the Chernobyl nuclear power station is a perfect example.

The investigation found that workers carried out an exceptional adaptation, a one-time breach of a work practice at the Chernobyl site. Staff deliberately ignored safety regulations and carried out a safety test too far. In this case, the goal was not to commit a malevolent act but actually to improve system safety. Professor James Reason explores the accident and provides another assessment. He writes that there are two cultural viewpoints that merit closer examination. On the one part, the Soviet nuclear power generation system seeded a culture that nuclear power was the *"ultimate in genuine safety, ecological cleanliness and reliability"* (Reason, 1998). The government would not release information on incidents or accidents, not even to the people who worked in the industry.

Grigori Medvedev, a prominent nuclear engineer who worked during the Soviet years, explains that there was *"a conspiracy of silence. Mishaps were never publicized; nobody knew about them, nobody could learn from them"* (Medvedev, 1991). For the purpose of this book, the second cultural viewpoint is more interesting; it has to do with the operators of the power plant. They had a blind confidence in the safety of their system and were actually prize-winners: the team had received an award for delivering the most kilowatts to the grid. The team bolstered this feeling of self-confidence, a culturally dangerous attitude attained because of their status as stars, similar to that of cosmonauts. Lastly, they displayed overconfidence: they believed they could handle anything. They were not afraid; they were arrogant; and they ignored the dangers. It all amounted to an unsafe organizational culture.

Professor Hofstede's work allowed a giant leap forward in the field of transport security. The Scandinavian Airline System (SAS) used his research to modify airline safety after the 1977 Los Rodeos disaster, instituting the first CRM course. Without his socio-logical research, we may still be producing investigation reports that merely recommend modifying cockpit or bridge procedures without knowing why. Today, investigation reports quote Hofstede to support recommendations to implement procedures and training of multicultural crews. CRM and BRM training goes beyond multicultural dynamics and incorporates other team dynamics also identified by other researchers.

Investigators need to understand why some cultures react differ-ently than others. Investigators should not claim that their view of the world or their view of the truth is the correct view. Socio-centrism, an identity retreat, which privileges one's own cultural values above all others can be a major flaw in one's perception of "normal" everyday behaviour. We investigate and see the truth according to our perspective, our beliefs, and our culture. For example, many of European descent do not consider knowledge-transfer based on word-of-mouth as a *bona fide* truth, a truth worth reporting. Indigenous people have a different point of view on this matter. Investigators need to adapt to their target audience if they want to improve safety. They have to know whom they are trying to reach and sell their truth, one point that I cover in more detail in the last chapter.

THE GYNOCENTRIC AND TRADITIONAL KNOWLEDGE LENSES

Starting in the late 1960s, feminist anthropologists began to explore the roles of women as described by anthropological data, data that was collected by teams led mostly by white males. At that time, there was an assumption of universal female subordination that pervaded anthropological theory. In the 1970s and '80s, more women became anthropologists, which brought about a rethink of the nature of this field of science. This period of development in anthropology was essential in questioning the academic white male point of view that had dominated anthropological thought. In 1975, Sally Slocum wrote an article entitled *Woman the Gatherer:*

Male Bias in Anthropology. It raises the question of the truth being gender biased. She sets the stage for her analysis with a few questions including *"What constitutes reality/knowledge/proof?"*

Today, many female anthropologists work to understand gender and power from a cultural perspective. Slocum posited, for example, that we had ignored women's roles in human evolution because scholars focused on hunting rather than gathering. She and others focused on gender inequality and what physical anthropologists called the "man the hunter" version of human evolution. Slocum argues that evidence indicates that foraging, not hunting, was the principal economic strategy throughout most of human evolution.

Charlotte Perkins Gilman (1869-1935) was a novelist, poet, a leading intellectual of the American women's movement, and lecturer for social reform. She introduced the term *androcentrism*, which refers to the practice, conscious or otherwise, of placing a masculine point of view at the centre of one's worldview, culture, and history, thereby culturally marginalizing femininity. We do not investigate how gender may influence work-as-done; we investigate using an androcentric point of view.

Slocum determined, after observing the protocol for bonobos and baboons, that anthropologists had a bias when they studied primates. We may truncate the truth when we observe with our own sexual bias. The truth is biased. It is natural to be biased. Each of us has our own view of things given our different experiences in life, and we all perceive the world differently. The important thing is that we become aware of this. That is what the field of anthropology has been doing, becoming aware of its biases and telling the world of its awareness.

Our gender does lead us to have specific attitudes, beliefs, and values. Behaviours of men and women can lead to unsafe practices. Let us just think about a man's reaction when called a sissy for wearing a safety harness. During my tenure as head of marine investigations, I held a few workshops to dig into our investigation process. One of these sessions involved two professors, Jessica Riel, from the Université du Québec en Outaouais, in Gatineau,

Quebec, and Nicole Power, from Memorial University in St. John's, Newfoundland and Labrador. Both professors are experts in the field of health and safety, with a particular interest in how we can learn from the feminist movement to understand occupational accidents. One of our takeaway messages from this session was that we need to understand the drivers of the behaviour (the change or the non-change), particularly values, beliefs, and attitudes.

We found that when it comes to the use of mobile devices while operating a vehicle, the research showed that communication is valued more highly than the risk associated with distracted driving. We found that male workers in several fields began to improve their safety behaviours after women started to be more prominent in traditionally male-dominated fields. Men often carry out unsafe practices; think about how many men did not wear safety equipment until it was made mandatory in the construction and logging industries. We found - without any statistical data, however - that women had a different approach to safety. Wearing safety equipment was not a problem for most women. When we examine the assumptions imbedded in work environments, such as "this harness is for weaklings, or sissies" we can conclude that we acquire social behaviour based on our own gender stereotypes.

After researching feminism and ecological social movements, I have come to realize the limits of the accident causation models used by investigators around the world. Earlier, we discussed how the simple linear and complex linear models are not very useful to help us understand values, beliefs, and attitudes. Investigators are not very good at understanding the underlying safety issues behind recurring high fatality levels in some industries, for example. We clearly need to use new theories, given that the traditional objectivist models and theories have not helped us shift systemic behaviours. I do not think any government, anywhere in the world, is properly equipped and prepared to study the impacts of the values, beliefs, and attitudes of their workers on health and safety. We need to study from the bottom-up; that is, start by studying the workers themselves. We need to think about researching unsafe practices. We also need to think more about gender attitudes and beliefs and cultural biases of all types, including those surrounding traditional Indigenous practices.

Indigenous knowledge is the accepted term for the beliefs and understandings that Indigenous Peoples acquired through long-term observation and association with a place. We also hear and use the term traditional knowledge. It is knowledge based on the social, physical, and spiritual understandings that informed Indigenous Peoples' survival.

The way of life and traditional knowledge of Indigenous People are crucial for their subsistence and even their survival. Traditional knowledge comes from the accumulation of empirical observation and daily interaction with the land. Traditional knowledge includes technologies of subsistence such as tools, ecological knowledge, traditional medicine, celestial navigation, and climate, to name a few. This knowledge passes orally from generation to generation. This knowledge is a form of truth.

Accident investigation is a relatively new practice that has only been around for a few decades. The work conducted is beneficial to society. However, we may have only identified the easiest systemic safety issues that exist in a worker's environment. We need to be more comprehensive. We need to look at the entire safety system - or absence of a safety system. The next step, and a bold step for traditional thinkers and governments, is to study the societal paradigm at the source of occupational accidents. We cannot improve safety if we do not understand why unsafe practices still prevail, why a deficient safety culture still prevails.

Our traditional scientific models are too circular. We need models that broaden our thinking. We probably need more scientists in the field of work-related accidents that focus on feminism and examine if we can learn from the ecological movement to induce new cultural attitudes and beliefs. We may need a new orientation of the economy and the social environment if we want to reshape the culture of our industries and reduce accidents at work. I actually believe the next frontier for improving safety is finding a way to ensure workers embrace practices that we can learn from the postmodern movements.

Investigators have not moved into the postmodern world. Postmodernism can be defined as an attitude of skepticism that calls into question assumptions of the certainty of Enlightenment. Common targets of postmodern critique include Universalist notions of reality, morality, reason, social progress, and truth! Postmodern thinkers call attention to socially conditioned nature of knowledge claims and value systems. Investigators could jump into the postmodern bandwagon by embracing a gynocentric investigation paradigm, a practice of placing the feminine point of view at the centre of our study.

We need to emulate movements that developed in the mid - to late-20th century across philosophy, the arts, and architecture. We need to embrace criticism that decided to go beyond modernism, understanding that what the modernists were doing was ill-fitted. In fact, this book can be said to be a postmodern approach to investigating failure as it confronts the ideological, social, and historical structures that shape and constrain the production of an investigation report. I reject the possibility of definitive knowledge when it comes to defining social behaviours in an industrial environment. I deny the existence of a universal and stable reality in our industrial environments. This does not mean that we cannot find a truth that can improve safety. This topic is covered in the next chapter.

In the concluding remarks, I attempt to explain the "whodunit effect," a postmodern way of thinking that I coined to help identify the infinite number of "culprits" that participate in the production of a disaster. I arrived at this theory pursuant to my failed attempts to convince members of my previous work environment in Canada and abroad that it is impossible to explain reality with objective certainty. Like postmodernists, I recognize that we construct reality as our minds try to understand our own personal circumstances and behaviours. This may be a difficult task as we are stuck in our world of certainty: We are still too comfortable with our traditional ways of investigating.

UNCOVERING HUMAN FACTORS

Perhaps you follow weekly investigations on your favourite web series or television show. You see the actions of police officers, but rarely get a glimpse into the logic process that culminated in the arrest of the culprit. If you are lucky, you might see an "org chart" on the wall showing the ugly faces of a criminal enterprise. Maybe a red marker shows you that there are some connections made by the team gathering evidence. Rarely do we see any semblance of the work carried out to find the guilty party. Often, this is difficult to portray visually, as the work takes place in one's mind or in several minds. You cannot always see an investigation pattern in novels either. My personal technique for writing is having my heroes find clues that I invent as the story goes and to zero in on a cause of death and villain. I use a model based on the simple linear and complex linear models we learned in the previous chapter. The heroes follow hints, hearsay, interviews, clues left on paperwork, etc. Finding a guilty party is part inquiry and part luck. The essential model for an investigation novel is that the reader should be able to build a linear model of how the murder came to be: they need to be able to line up the dominoes.

If you are investigating an industrial accident, you are not searching for a culprit. Instead, you want to understand the human factors that led to the occurrence or disaster. The model used by most investigators integrates a number of human-factor frameworks: SHELL *(Hawkins, 1987)* and Reason's (1990) Accident Causation and generic error-modelling system (GEMS) frameworks, as well as Rasmussen's Taxonomy of Error (1987). Let me emphasize one more time: Theoretical models are not investigation techniques. Theoretical models give investigators guidance to develop methodical insights circumscribing how accidents happen.

Accidents happen because humans develop imperfect work environments. The work of investigators is to uncover the human factors that lead to an accident. The first step in the human factors investigation process is the collection of work-related information regarding the personnel, tasks, equipment, and environmental conditions involved in the occurrence. A systematic approach to this step is crucial to ensure that a comprehensive analysis is possible and that we meet the logistical requirements of collecting, organizing, and maintaining a relevant occurrence-related database. To conduct an effective systematic collection of data, the investigator must recognize from the outset that workplaces (e.g., a cockpit or a control tower) are parts of larger "work systems," with each system consisting of varied and interrelated elements, i.e., human, task, equipment, and environmental elements.

For complex systems, where there are numerous interactions between the component elements, there is a constant danger that we will overlook or lose critical information during an investigation. When investigators use the SHELL model as an organizational tool to collect data in the workplace, they are less likely to face analytical problems downstream. Before analyzing the data, you must properly collect it. Investigators take into consideration all the important work system elements, they consider the interrelationships between the work system elements, and they focus on the factors that influence human performance by relating all of the peripheral elements to the central element called liveware.

The investigation process initially attempts to answer the more simplistic questions concerning "what, who, and when," and then moves to more complicated questions of "how and why." The resulting data becomes, for the most part, a collection of events and circumstances comprised of acts and conditions. Some of these will be unsafe acts and unsafe conditions. As the investigator moves to addressing questions of "how and why," there is a need to link the data identified in the first step of the process. This is the second step.

In practice, step 1 (data gathering, answering the questions, "what, who, and when") and step 2 (producing a sequence of events) may not be mutually exclusive. As investigators begin the data collection step, it would be only natural that they attempt to place the information, albeit often fragmentary in the preliminary stages of an investigation, into the context of an occurrence sequence. To facilitate this concurrent activity, investigators can combine the SHELL and Reason models.

Then the investigator may apply (I say may, as most investigators in most countries don't use the following process) a framework based upon Reason's Accident Causation and generic error-modelling system (GEMS) and Rasmussen's Taxonomy of Error. The framework provides "pathways" that lead from the identification of the unsafe act/decision to the identification of what was erroneous about the action or decision and finally to its placement within a behavioural context, a failure mode within a given level of performance. Let me describe these in more detail.

You want to identify unsafe acts, unsafe decisions, and unsafe conditions. To do so, the investigation takes on a reductionist nature whereby the investigator gathers and organizes information using the SHELL and Reason frameworks to initiate identification of occurrence causal factors, the unsafe acts/decisions and conditions. Reason, as we have seen, defines an unsafe act as an error or adaptation (modification of a rule or plan, or a calculated adjustment) that is committed in the presence of a hazard or potential unsafe condition. Decisions, where there are no apparent resulting actions, but which have a negative impact on safety, should also be considered as unsafe acts. An unsafe condition, or hazard, is an event or circumstance that has the potential to result in a mishap. There may be several acts, decisions, and/or conditions that are potential unsafe candidates. This means we need to do iterative assessments of the occurrence facts.

When you identify an unsafe act, decision, or condition, the focus shifts to determining the genesis of that particular act or condition. Further investigation and/or analysis may reveal other unsafe acts/decisions or conditions antecedent to the causal factor that was initially identified.

As noted earlier, you may have already identified, during the first steps, several unsafe acts and decisions. The last unsafe act precipitating the occurrence often provides a convenient starting point for reconstruction of the occurrence. This last act or decision differs from the others, in that it can be viewed as the definitive action or decision that led to the occurrence. We determine what we believe was the last act or decision that made the accident or incident inevitable. Although it is usually an active failure, the last unsafe act or decision can be embedded in a latent unsafe condition, such as a flawed design decision that led to a system failure.

You now want to identify the error or adaptation type. This process is initiated for each unsafe act/decision by posing the simple question, "What is erroneous or wrong about the action or decision that eventually made it unsafe?" This involves two sub-steps. First, it is necessary to determine whether the error or adaptation was an unintentional or intentional action. For example, "Did you expect your action to produce the effects it did?" If the answer to that question is "no," then it is an unintentional action. Unintentional actions are actions that do not go as planned. You made an execution error. If the answer to the question "Did you expect your action to produce the effects it did?" is "yes," then the action is intentional. Intentional actions are actions that you planned, but the actions are inappropriate; these are planning errors.

In the second sub-step, you select the error type or adaptation that best describes the failure, keeping in mind the decision regarding intentionality. Again, as we have seen, there are four potential error/adaptation categories: a slip, a lapse, a mistake, and an adaptation. We covered this already in Chapter I, but let me remind you by summarizing. A slip is an unintentional action where the failure involves attention. These are errors in execution. A lapse is an unintentional action where the failure involves memory. These are also errors in execution. A mistake is an intentional action, but there is no deliberate decision to act against a rule or plan. These are errors in planning. An adaptation is a planning failure where you made a deliberate decision to act against a rule or plan.

On 22 January 2016, the container vessel MSC *Monica* ran aground in the St. Lawrence River in Quebec, Canada. The vessel sustained minor damage to the hull and major damage to the four propeller blades. The following is an example of how you can describe errors identified in your second sub-step using the sequence of events you created.

The MSC *Monica* unexpectedly veered to starboard and exited a buoyed channel. Testing and examinations established that the steering gear and its control system were fully functional and that no steering failure occurred. The winds and current were not strong enough to cause the vessel's path to change, and the vessel's speed was not excessive for this particular type of vessel in this section of the river.

The results of the investigation demonstrated that the most plausible scenario for causing the vessel to veer was the helm being inadvertently placed to starboard. Upon observing the course deviation, the helmsman said to the pilot, *"Not working."* However, this expression is ambiguous; it can be interpreted to mean that the system has failed or that there is insufficient steering. When the pilot asked, *"It's not responding?"* the helmsman replied, *"It's not."* The pilot and the officer of the watch concluded that the steering gear had failed based on their interpretation of the helmsman's responses. The pilot was unaware of the informal shipboard practice for the helmsman to warn the bridge team whenever the need to apply more than 10 degrees of rudder to keep the vessel on course was necessary. The practice was understood by the master, the navigation officers, and the helmsmen, but was not documented nor was it communicated to the pilot.

Even though this was a time-critical situation, the bridge team did not communicate well and concluded that there was a steering gear failure without working together to verify the failure or consider other alternatives; this is consistent with groupthink. Alarmed by the developing situation, the pilot ordered the crew to switch to an alternate steering system. With the need to take immediate action, the pilot proceeded to switch to the alternate steering and do it himself. The pilot did not know that the alternate steering system was installed in the inverse position, not in accordance with the manufacturer's specifications. Thus, he unintentionally applied a helm order on the wrong side, and the vessel exited the channel and ran aground. (TSB, M16C0005)

Routine adaptations occur every day, as most of us regularly modify or do not strictly comply with work procedures, often because of poorly designed or defined work practices. As an investigator, you need to identify the relationship between the occurrence errors/ adaptations and the behaviour that led to them. This requires extensive and time-consuming effort. Your investigation work starts with excellent interviews and information gathered at the site of the occurrence. We do not normally say evidence, as we are not searching for a guilty party, but what we are doing is collecting data. The data can come from objects, documents, and, if you are lucky, electronic data (video and other recorders like voyage data recorders, better known as black boxes… which are never black but generally orange, by the way). The presence of electronic data is the case now in most major industrial accidents. When you return to the office, you need to identify and separate activities. You may have to do this in an arbitrary way since you may not know exactly what took place first. You just write everything down, keeping in mind a behaviour consists of a decision and an action or movement.

So you, the investigator, identified the action or decision (i.e., unsafe act or decision). Then you found what was erroneous regarding that action or decision. You now place your focus on the decision that eventually led to the erroneous action or decision. The investigator accomplishes this by placing the errors (slips, lapses, and mistakes) and adaptations into the context of performance (behaviour). In other words, you determine how the worker performed at the time of the failure.

You just focused on the identification of failure modes, which described erroneous decision-making or unsafe acts. To uncover the underlying causes behind the decision of a worker or group of workers, it is important to determine if there were any factors in the work system that may have facilitated the expression of the given failure mode (and hence the error/adaptation and the unsafe act). We call these factors behavioural antecedents. You can find them by examining the work system information collected and organized using the SHELL or Reason frameworks that you used in the beginning of your investigation, in steps 1 and 2, if you prefer. The re-examination of these data again emphasizes the iterative nature of this investigative process. It is important to re-examine, as you may, once again in the process, deem it necessary to conduct further investigation work into the occurrence. You constantly go back and close the loop. We can actually see a parallel form of this being done on television-or on Internet for those on streaming-when an investigator is looking at a wall plastered with a flowchart containing pictures and hints.

Once we are satisfied with our investigation, we get into the final step. We identify potential safety problems. This is based extensively on the factors that were identified as behavioural antecedents. Once again, this underscores the importance of the application of a systematic approach to steps 1 and 2 of the process, which sets the foundation for the subsequent analysis steps.

KNOWING WHAT DID NOT HAPPEN

Investigators do not cover non-events, actions not carried out but that, if done, would have changed the course of the event. (An example of a non-event is stopping your vehicle when fatigued and handing over the driving to the passenger of your automobile, something you did not do which resulted in you falling asleep and crashing the vehicle.) This was one of the first things I learned when I became the head of an investigation body. My managers and staff would take turns setting me straight. I withheld my frustration and carried on. They had the wisdom. I now believe they were correct, but only because they were repeating what they were taught. The investigation methodology is flawed. You also need to study non-events.

Investigators uncover events that happened using an epidemiological investigation methodology. This allows you to determine if the work carried out was as the work-is-imagined. If you want to understand how the work-is-done, you need to look at the performance. This means understanding non-events. As I covered previously, *"We lack models based on what people actually do, on the recurrent patterns of behaviour"* (Hollnagel, 2016). We should not just analyze the work-as-planned, but also the work-in-practice. This requires understanding the complex adaptive behaviour and the practices. To tell the story of this complexity, we also need to state what did not happen, a definitive "no-no" in traditional investigation work.

Investigation outfits and organizations interested in digging deeper and examining team dynamics, such as language issues or other social safety issues connected to cultural background, need to resort to methods other than the classic simple linear and complex linear models. Investigators essentially draw conclusions on how the work-is-done based on how the work-was-imagined. They rarely analyze why the work-as-done was done the way it was. This is where an investigator needs to pass the ball to an ergonomist, a fatigue management specialist, or another human factors expert who can dig into the various social, health, psychological, economic, and political problems that provide the context for an accident. Some of these problems were identified in the first sections of this chapter (socially induced errors) and in the last section of the first chapter (human performance). An investigation can then take on a new life that lasts as long as we want to study the issue or the social, economic or political system. We can then discover many new truths and many new avenues to improve safety.

If you are on your own as a solo investigator, you need to be cognizant that the governing principle behind a behaviour, behind performance, is not causality but rather resonance - the phenomenon that relates to the general stability of the system or from its various interactions. You need to understand the various interactions and outcomes that emerge and lead to the unexpected and unintended combination of performance variability. You can achieve this by first throwing away the idea that you are not looking for non-events. You actually should include questions such as "What could have happened?" in your interviews of accident survivors. Presently, investigators limit their interview questions to learn about linear causation, the epidemiological story that always starts with "Tell me the story of what happened."

Investigative interviewing is the same for all types of investigations. The procedures are largely based on "cognitive interviewing," a method that uses scientific principles of memory and communication. The method is a systematic approach to maximize the amount of information one can elicit from an interviewee. Investigators are taught to ask questions such as "Would you or could you have done anything differently?" "What should be done to correct/prevent the occurrence from happening again?" and, "What would you like to see to improve safety?" However, since these questions can lead to the description of non-events, they are either not asked or discarded when the investigator recreates the sequence of events.

CLOSING ARGUMENTS

This book does not cover all of the different tasks involved in an investigation. However, it is important that I mention that I do not think that the training and techniques, including training to conduct interviews, properly prepare investigators to tell the story of the various performances that may have prevented the accident. Investigators train to find reasons and causes. Investigators should also be trained to find patterns and sociological, environmental, and economic factors that lead to unexpected and unintended performance failure. When investigators realize that they are not equipped to carry out the task of uncovering or studying a human science safety issue related to behaviours or performance, they should be able to identify that they need help. This is not something that one can learn, especially if one suffers the inevitable impression that they found the truth using the simple or complex linear investigation methodologies.

By now, we have circled the wagons. We are in a position to extract findings. We can now list what we believe are the causes, contributing factors, and risks in the work environment that resulted in an accident. We are now in a position to construct a story with the facts that have been uncovered. We can now tell everyone how we saw this accident unfolding. It is now your opinion of what happened.

Remember, you can go back in time as far as you think necessary to explain how this accident was created. It will be your version of the truth, your truth. Investigators are translators of a sort, helping society understand and explain the gaps between how work is carried out and how it is imagined. You need to remember that investigators can get close to the truth, but they need to remain humble and cognizant that their understanding of how work-is-done is limited and will never be complete.

IV

Reality Check
Seeking and Debating the Truth

LOOKING FOR CLUES

> › *Intersubjective view of the world*
> › *Constant evolution of true science*
> › *Positivism has its negative side*
> › *Accumulating knowledge versus sharing wisdom*
> › *Emotional purpose of investigations*

It was the morning of 14 October 2014, in the Canadian Arctic, west of Deer Island in the Chesterfield Inlet, Nunavut. There was no daylight yet, autumn had set, and ice had started to infest the cold waters. The tanker *Nanny* was exiting a narrow waterway and heading south after delivering fuel to remote villages for the upcoming winter.

The captain was on the bridge of the ship. He was tired and looking forward to a good sleep. He planned to get some shuteye after he made the next couple of course changes. Morning twilight was close, and daylight would make navigation easier. He would hand over the ship to his trustworthy second in command who was currently snoring and enjoying a good dream.

The vessel was underway in the confined waters at full speed ahead, making 16.7 knots and moving in the same direction as the ebb tide. The master was looking at the radar; the outside sky was pitch black, and heavy clouds prevented the northern lights from dancing for the crew. The horizon showed a glimmer of red: the sun wanting to show its face. The lookout was scrutinizing the horizon. He was not much help in assisting with identifying navigational hazards - his main task - as there was no traffic to report to the watch officer and it was impossible to identify any hazards because the forward projector lights were showing frozen water, a glaze of grey-white and bluish colour, along with the occasional ice patch that would pop up. The officer of the watch checked the radar occasionally and logged the vessel's position. The bridge team was completed by a helmsman. All were fatigued from the watch and several poor sleeps while off watch.

The vessel was being steered from a central helm station situated slightly aft of the bridge centre console. The vessel had three rudder angle indicators: one at the helm position, one on the centre console between the radars, and one mounted on the ceiling of the bridge, slightly aft of the port radar.

Chesterfield Inlet is a 124-nautical-mile navigational waterway that joins Baker Lake, a freshwater lake, to Hudson Bay. The community of Baker Lake is 40 nautical miles from its western entrance to the inlet. Strong tidal streams of three to five knots cause cross-currents in much of the waterway. Ebb tide flows of up to eight knots have been reported in the Chesterfield Narrows, and tidal rips are frequent at Deer Island channel. The shallowest point of the inlet is 4.2 metres, at the narrows.

Climate change has modified the navigational season in the Arctic. Vessels are now plying the waters much earlier in the spring and much later in the fall. There are many unlit land-based aids to navigation and many areas with scarce visual aids. Therefore, crews cannot generally use visual aids to navigation, the most accurate and reliable method to navigate. Ranges are two land-based pillars, separated by a certain distance that, once lined up, provide the navigator with a safe line for navigation. Further south where there is heavy traffic, ranges have electric-powered lights to facilitate night pilotage.

Twilight was still a short time away. The inlet is one nautical mile wide or slightly narrower, except for three course legs where the channel broadens to two nautical miles or more. On the approaches to Baker Lake, the navigable width of the inlet narrows to less than 100 metres, which is very tight to lead a ship, especially without buoys. Transiting the inlet requires making over 50 course alterations, 12 of which are greater than 70 degrees, a large course change for such a narrow waterway. Piloting the waterway at night is a challenging and monotonous task.

The landscape around the Chesterfield Inlet is low and sloping, with few distinguishing features. The shores are rocky and the radar images they produce correspond well with the charts. There are 17 unlit leading beacon ranges that mark the route through Chesterfield Inlet. Two of these ranges mark the outbound (easterly) route through Deer Island Channel. Transiting vessels sometimes transit during darkness because they can only pass through Chesterfield Narrows during high tide, which occurs about every 12 hours.

Fifty years ago, when the 17 ranges were installed to mark the route through Chesterfield Inlet, there was no need for lights, as there was no night navigation. The waters were covered with ice in October, rendering navigation too dangerous. The Canadian Coast Guard (CCG) put these aids to navigation in place in the 1960s to facilitate pilotage through this passage, which is amongst the most difficult waters to pilot in the country. Aids to navigation are critical, especially in these dangerous areas. The CCG knew this but had not adapted the waterway to consider change brought about by a longer navigational season.

The *Nanny* was approaching a turn with the next set of ranges on the port side a few miles ahead. Nobody on the bridge could see them given darkness. The captain was about to announce a course change to port. He looked at the chart and saw the set of land-based ranges that, if it were daylight, he would have to line up with the vessel. They were about to be lined up with an imaginary line that he could trace on the radar. He was also able to follow the vessel on an electronic chart system that showed the ranges and the position of the vessel.

In daylight, the master would have been on the port side of the vessel, looking at the ranges closing with his binoculars, noting the most appropriate time to alter course. At nighttime, he was behind the radar, waiting a bit longer before giving the helmsman the order to alter course to port. This is how work-is-done for professional pilots: they want to use the visual aids and align themselves as close as possible to the target they use to turn. A few more seconds elapsed, and then the captain said "Port 20." The helmsman heard the order, repeated "Port 20," but mistakenly altered course to starboard. The captain repeated "Port 20," which was the normal procedure, but did not check the rudder angle and did not see the helmsman accidentally altering course to starboard.

The captain checked the radar and saw the vessel's heading change to starboard. He thought the current and wind were pushing the vessel in that direction and ordered more rudder angle: "Hard to port." The helmsman repeated the order and proceeded to turn the rudder full starboard. Moments later, the vessel started turning rapidly. The master approached the central helm station and saw that the rudder angle order was set to hard to starboard (30 degrees). As he got nearer, he informed the helmsman that he had the rudder set on the wrong side. However, by that time, it was too late. The vessel grounded with a racket that jolted awake all of the crew on the ship.

I got a call from my duty officer shortly after the accident, after the master reported the grounding to his owner and the CCG. It was *déjà vu* all over again. The tanker had also grounded in the inlet on October 25, 2012, two years earlier. I was also the director of investigations at that time.

The vessel was not taking on water and there was no apparent breach in the hull. We gathered a multidisciplinary team and developed an investigation plan. Our minds got to work. We thought about making our way up north, but once there, we had no way to reach the ship in the inlet. We therefore started the investigation from a distance and prepared to board the vessel upon its arrival in Newfoundland.

The team started data gathering and prepared to conduct interviews. It was time for my team and I to put ourselves in the shoes of the members of the bridge team. It was time for me to provide direction, to help the team understand some issues I wanted them to investigate.

* * *

THE INVESTIGATOR'S MAZE

In the three previous mazes, we sketched out the various steps that allow you to develop a report that comprises three sections, a factual, an analysis, and findings. We assume for the purpose of this maze and relevant to the theories being examined in this chapter, that you now have completed a draft report that has gone into the hands of team members. We may have integrated the work of social scientists, physicians (e.g., evidence of sleep apnea), laboratories (e.g., drug or alcohol consumption; metallurgy or mechanical failure; etc.) and various human factors specialists. Our work does not end there.

We have a story, but we may not all agree on the safety messages. We may not all agree on the story, either. In most investigation bodies, the investigation team reports to a director or a chief inspector who in return may report to a board or a commission, to name a few examples. In large investigation outfits, there are various steps in the approval process. The published report may differ from the draft produced by the investigator-in-charge. The report goes through several iterations, including various levels of approval culminating in a penultimate copy produced by the board or commission which is submitted to the companies, various actors (workers) and witnesses to allow them to confirm or provide information they believe has been improperly reported.

During these various stages of internal approval, it is wise to go back to the sequence of events. It is imperative that you do this if there are diverging opinions - and these are inevitable in every stage of the development of a report. You need to agree or at least find some common ground on what are the salient unsafe acts, unsafe decisions, and unsafe conditions. In order to do so, and since the ultimate goal is to produce the safety messages that will render the best safety outcomes and protect the environment, you may need to go back to some questions generated by the director, the chief inspector or the investigator-in-charge prior to the deployment. For this scenario, I provide a sample of questions that could have been developed prior to the deployment at the *Nanny*'s port of call.

· Why was the tanker leaving the Arctic so late in the season?

· How was the team working together?

· Was the crew fatigued?

· Why did the vessel miss the turn?

· Could the bridge team rely on aids to navigation?

* * *

WHO HOLDS THE TRUTH?

To ensure effective monitoring of a vessel's progress in confined waters, navigators use a combination of navigational equipment and visual aids to navigation. This assists in maintaining situational awareness with respect to the vessel's progress and allows for cross-checking to identify potential equipment or human errors. In restricted waters, of which there are many in Arctic areas, we monitor the vessel's position through a combination of visual references such as leading lines, headmarks, and buoy/beacons used together with one or two radars. If you do not have visual references, you have got yourself a hefty challenge. In fact, no vessel should be allowed to navigate waters without a proper navigational aid system.

In confined waters, the navigator's task becomes more challenging, especially when frequent course changes are necessary. A higher workload results in less time to attend to other required duties of the watch, such as position plotting, logbook keeping, radio communications, and monitoring of other bridge team members. In these circumstances, it is common for the master and another officer to share the responsibilities. At any given point, the navigator needs a backup - someone else who is monitoring the progress of the vessel and is ready to act - as there may be little time to respond to a navigational error or an emergency. In the case of the *Nanny*, the master had the con, which is marine terminology to say that he was the one giving the orders and in charge of piloting while supported by the other bridge team members who shared the duties and were responsible for cross-checking the piloting.

In this occurrence, the master was on the bridge with the officer of the watch. The captain was navigating through confined waters in accordance with on-board practices. We are not in a very challenging situation, as there is no other vessel traffic, and there is a simple course change to make. The captain only needed to make a simple pilotage manoeuvre, a manoeuvre I have made thousands of times in my career on the bridge with a helmsman and a lookout - and with proper aids to navigation, which was not the case in this geographical area.

The investigation report mentions poor navigational procedures as one of the causes of the grounding. Fatigue was a contributory factor. The findings also identify inadequate pilotage by the bridge team members, pointing out that their procedures were not adequate to effectively navigate the vessel. These are accurate findings: no investigation team in any investigation body in the world would dispute these findings. However, if the bridge team does not have appropriate aids to navigation, then how can they do their job properly? What is the truth that we need to tell the public in order to prevent similar accidents from happening? How would the work-as-done differ if there were proper aids to navigation? We do not know and do not investigate, as this is a non-event.

Investigators do not examine non-events *(see Chapter III)* when they use epidemiological models. Non-events are a no-no, shot down by the investigation team when someone dares identify one in the sequence of events. "Why did the captain miss the turn?" is not answered by "Because he did not have range lights?" or "Because he was not standing on the port side" (The helmsman would have seen the captain with his binoculars looking at the ranges, providing a strong indication to the fatigued crew member that the turn had to be made towards the master, to port. He would also have heard the captain say his orders out loud from the port side). Instead the investigation team may answer that the captain missed the turn because of his ineffective navigation, because he was fatigued, or because of poor bridge teamwork.

Ineffective navigation of a vessel is not an earth-shattering finding. Raising the concern and informing the public that the Arctic lacks navigational aids in this time of increased traffic is a much better message, a key message that remains relevant as you read these lines. One fundamental principle for safe pilotage of vessels is that the crew must use proper visual aids. This is the way work-is-done safely. If there are no aids to navigation, the crew is lacking a most basic means to ensure safe navigation, especially if they are fatigued. We can draw many truths from this investigation: one is a game changer; the others are knowledge that has little chance of improving safety in the Arctic. Why can we have different answers?

The first reason is that investigators obtusely believe they have to use epidemiological accident models without being aware of their often-poor interpretative capacity to translate how work-is-done. They do not cover non-events. They do not tell a story of how the work-as-imagined differed from the way we would carry out work if there were proper navigational aids. The second reason, which is closely related to the first, is that an accident report is the result of a team piecing together a story they construct according to their subjective views, after having collected facts also influenced by their subjective views. We can never eliminate bias.

An investigation team often comprises individuals with different opinions and experiences. These individuals also often have different training. The contents of investigation reports are not objective phenomena that exist independently of human perspectives and beliefs. Therefore, the social construct of an accident that leads to the identification of causes and contributing factors is always the result of one's own perspective and beliefs. A report derives from the intersubjective views - the common perspective and belief - of an investigation network and becomes a collection of the subjective perspectives of many individuals linked together. The report remains true, but primarily for the investigation team.

You can access the investigation reports and read about both times the tanker *Nanny* grounded in the Arctic. Nobody disputes the findings. However, we need to ask ourselves what we want our goal to be. Do we want to share information based on intersubjective views that will have little impact on improving safety? Do we want to focus the report to achieve robust results? The authority responsible for endorsing and publishing investigation reports needs to share knowledge that will provide the best results.

We need to start investigations by agreeing on common perspectives and beliefs. This would bring into play the fact that vessels operating in the Arctic and Antarctic face a number of unique risks such as extreme weather conditions. Also, it is a challenge for mariners to pilot these waters given the relative lack of good charts, communication systems, and navigational aids. This is well-known information that should be part of the common consciousness of the investigation team and the authority endorsing the reports. We need to communicate the knowledge that will improve safety. Investigators can only achieve this if their subjective view is accepted by the community - the network building the investigation report - and those responsible for endorsing and publishing the findings.

Philosophers tell us that well-informed people, acting in good faith, might have a profound disagreement on the same topic. This applies to the investigative world as well, where there are many truths and no absolute truth. Some knowledge gleaned during an investigation can shift the manner in which we produce and manage work environments; some knowledge goes into oblivion.

I will now take you on a short journey to show you that the truth can take various forms, as in the accident where the tanker *Nanny* grounded in the Canadian Arctic. We can produce different understandings of these accidents. I will show you that investigators need to know that there is both rational and emotional knowledge. The former is what most investigation bodies concern themselves with; they apply a methodology to determine findings using rational knowledge. The latter is what scientists use to inform the first; they start - should start - by determining what they desire to understand. This is an absolute necessity; it should be at the basis of reasoning and producing rational knowledge. For Arctic navigation, we may want to start by desiring to help mariners reduce the risk of piloting in treacherous waters.

The next section of this chapter covers a literature review about the truth, about searching for the truth, and about searching for answers in the various fields of science. The same concepts apply to searching for causes and contributing factors in industrial accidents. I will show you how searching for evidence and producing knowledge about accidents involves the same challenges as those encountered in evidence-based science research. The last section of this chapter expands on the idea of producing knowledge for the benefit of humankind by instilling the notion of emotional purpose in our investigations.

TRUE SCIENCE... TRUE STORY?

Nicolaus Copernicus lay in bed in the tower of a cathedral in Frombork, Poland. Heating was not even a luxury in the beginning of the 16th century, and it was cold. He had arranged the room in the tower so that he could live and make observations of the stars. Warmly clothed, he thought about his recent findings on astronomy. He wanted to tell the truth to the world, at least to the world as it was known at that time. His findings were irrefutable; he was the custodian of the truth. A new truth. The Earth was not the centre of the universe. Was he right?

Copernicus conducted research in the field of astronomy; this was the Renaissance-era mathematician and astronomer's main occupation. He formulated a model that placed the Sun rather than the Earth, at the centre of the universe, most probably independently of Aristarchus of Samos, who had formulated the same model some 18 centuries earlier. He convinced himself of the need to abandon the Ptolemaic universe model in favour of a heliocentric system. From the years 1511-13, he wrote a short treatise that exposed the heliocentric system. He was prudent not to share his findings. He secretly circulated a manuscript to his friends only. For 36 years, by his own admission, Copernicus kept his thought to himself without revealing it. His reason for doing so, however, was probably based more in scientific rigour than in awareness of the dangers of publishing such an idea. Circulating the truth could be dangerous, but it is interesting to note that, even back then, scientific rigour was already a pillar amongst researchers. Copernicus called into question the truth of certain dogmas of the church when he proposed the heliocentric system. In fact, he opposed revelation with a truth that was supported by scientific evidence.

Today, there is an extensive study of the truth, or that which constitutes true science. The Canadian philosopher Étienne Groleau paints a fascinating portrait of the "problem of truth" in his book *L'oubli de la vie* (2018). In our modern world, and probably since the beginning of the human era, man has had a great quest: finding the truth. This is especially the case for the Socratics, for whom the truth is subordinate to the good. We are constantly thinking about the truth. Truth is an ancient concept that grew out of Aristotelian logic. Absolute truth is one of the dogmas of determinism as we have seen in Chapter II. The idea that one person, one religion, or one state possesses the "One Truth" has been one of the most destructive ideas in the history of thought.

Philosophical truths can be divided into four categories. We can have truth by correspondence (with the external world) that we also qualify as synthetic (a posteriori) truth, or what David Hume and Gottfried Wilhelm Leibniz, two prominent philosophers would qualify as "matters of fact." There is also truth by consistency (internal to logic), which is also known as analytic (a priori) truth, or truth by definition of terms, sometimes circular and tautological. Hume would say, "relationship of ideas" and Leibniz would say, "truths of reason." Thirdly, we have truth by coherence (of logic and the world). Finally, there is pragmatic truth, attributed to beliefs that have practical consequences, as agreed upon by an open community of inquirers over a long period of time.

The idea of a fixed absolute timeless truth implies that we know and determine everything. However, nothing is that true in the world. We even hold scientific truths for a provisional period of time, subject to further experiments. An example is the shift to a heliocentric universe from a belief that we lived in a geocentric universe. Nothing is logically true, and nothing is physically certain. We can determine the truth within logic, but finding a logical explanation is, at best, limited and uncertain.

We continue to pursue our quest for the truth about our place in the universe. Scientists have questioned heliocentrism since the Middle Ages. We now know that the Sun is not the centre of the universe. It is from modernity - let us fix this period after the Renaissance to facilitate the argument - that reason holds the chief place in our explanation of the world. We started to replace science in lieu of religion and God as the answer for everything. In fact, since we have the ability to explain divine mysteries, we should rationally conclude that God does not exist. That is the reasoning. Today's truths are the result of objective analysis using instruments, methods, measurements, and calculations.

There are many more examples of scientific truths that end up not being exactly what we thought. I studied biology during my college years. At the beginning of one class, the professor queried us on the various theories of evolution. Someone started by stating the biblical theory. He is correct; it is a theory, but we did not go any further than listing it in class. We spent most of the time discussing the views of two scientists who did not believe in the biblical theories to explain how life evolved from a few simple organisms into many more complex organisms.

Charles Darwin (1809-82) and Jean-Baptiste de Lamarck (1744-1829) both thought that all living things had changed gradually over time and were still changing. They both believed that the change was driven by an imperative to become better adapted to their environments. They also believed that all organisms are related. Darwin proposed that changes in species occurred due to breeding. Survival came from genetic changes that helped some species to adapt better to the new conditions. Species that died were unable to adapt.

Lamarck held that species underwent changes in response to changes in their environment. The changes were permanent for as long as the new environmental conditions continued to apply. We laughed at Lamarck's theory in class, with students joking that if we left a dirty rag in a corner for a few months, this could eventually lead to a bug living inside it to become a rat. We were in fact, mistakenly, comparing his theory to the old Aristotelian idea, spontaneous generation, a concept that both Darwin and Lamarck were striving to replace with their own ideas.

Darwin won. We now speak about natural selection and survival of the fittest. That would be the truth. However, we are now rehabilitating Lamarck, some 200 years later. The bad jokes we made may be on us. While we agree that Darwin's theory of evolution is the "true" understanding of the origin of the diversity of life, there is also some truth to Lamarck's assertion that a species can evolve over the course of a lifetime.

The classical example used to explain Lamarck's theory is that of the giraffe. The species had to strive for leaves higher up in the trees, so its neck stretched. The offspring consequently had longer necks. Darwin suggested that random mutations produced individuals with longer necks, affording them better survival than those with smaller necks. We still hold Darwin's view as the correct view. However, researchers are now striving to understand the epigenetic code that consists of chemical modifications to the DNA and to the proteins that associate with and package DNA. Modifications occur over an organism's lifetime and regulate gene expression, sometimes for the better and other times for the worse. Some changes will be transient, while some will be permanent.

Interestingly, scientists have found, in recent years, that parents can pass on changes to their offspring. This is known as transgenerational epigenetic inheritance, the transmission of information from one generation to the next, affecting the traits of the offspring without alteration of the primary structure of DNA (Heard and Martienssen, 2014). For some traits, we now know that the environment induces epigenetic marks. Lamarck was not so wrong after all. He was correct in stating a principle of intergenerational inheritance, even though he had not and was not able to determine the order of complexity in his theory.

Changes like this also happen in the fields of social and political sciences, but perhaps in a less dramatic way. Robert David Putnam is an American political scientist from the Harvard University

John F. Kennedy School of Government. He is the author of the famous work *Bowling Alone, The Collapse and Revival of American Community* (2000), which argued that the USA inherited serious problems following the collapse in civic, social, associational, and political life, which we also call social capital, around the middle of the last century. He described the reduction of in-person social interaction, traditionally used to bond, educate, and enrich the fabric of social lives. He argued that this reduction in social inter-action undermined active civil engagement that, in turn, negatively affected the country's democracy. Fifteen years later, in 2015, he published an article noting that the trend had moved the other way. He concluded that his now-famous thesis was no longer true.

How does this understanding of truth as an ever-evolving concept impact the implementation of policies, investigations into accidents, and other social processes? Is there something that we can call evidence-based policymaking or true findings when we just demonstrated that the truth is ever evolving? That the evidence is ever evolving? How do we reconcile ourselves with the subjectivity in producing accident reports? Is there a *bona fide* process, a foolproof process, a bulletproof process to ensure that we uncover the appropriate causes, contributing factors, and risks in industrial accidents?

In the field of accident investigations, the authorities responsible for publishing accident reports are perceived as the custodians of the truth. They determine, by whichever process they want to put in place, what they believe to be the truth they want to communicate. They determine what they want the public to know. They are the custodians of your safety. They have the last say, just like a coroner or health and safety board in your jurisdiction. We can debate the truth, and the truth can have different versions. It can emerge from a cognitive process, or it can result from an authority that bases conclusions on embodied cultural practices with historical enablers and conditions.

THERE'S A LIMIT TO POSITIVISM

Over a period of about 100 years, bringing us to the end of the Second World War, we count the creation of six of the social science disciplines in major universities: sociology, economics, anthropology, history, oriental studies and political science. Then, the boundaries fall from these institutionalized disciplines and different faculties start to emerge, including industrial relations, a field in which I have interrupted doctoral research that led to this essay.

The natural sciences no longer solely occupy the central terrain. In fact, there was a rapprochement of the natural sciences and the social sciences. We can understand this phenomenon when we study contemporary epistemological evolution that comprises four concepts: positivism, neo-positivism, sophisticated neo-positivism, and conventionalism. I will explain this further.

Positivism is the conception that reality is measurable, tactile, and visible. The scientist has nothing to do with the construction of the object they are examining. A researcher finds, proves, or refutes. Positivism encompasses the notion of quantifiable truth, that which we derive from universal laws. Neo-positivism comprises two epistemological positions, empiricism and logic. In the first position (empiricism), researchers consider themselves as external observers to their object of study. They develop assumptions and then experiment to draw conclusions in an objective manner without involving their personal values or interests. Science follows its course by accumulating knowledge and searching for universal laws. In the second position (logic), science would be neither certain nor precise, as would have said Karl Popper (Fuller, 2006). The research proceeds through experimentation and researchers base their research on arbitrary rules. Theories are not absolute, but once accepted by the community of scientists, they will be considered the best available.

Two other concepts emerged from critics of neo-positivism: the conventionalism associated with Michael Polanyi and Thomas Kuhn, and "sophisticated" neo-positivism associated with Imre Lakatos. The three of them made significant contributions in the field of philosophy. Lakatos was a Hungarian who was known for his thesis of the fallibility of mathematics and its methodology of proofs and refutations. Sophisticated neo-positivism is a concept whereby scientists have a subjective attachment to their research program. Lakatos believed that it is wrong to say that a new theory would sweep away past knowledge.

Polanyi was a Hungarian-British thinker who argued that positivism is a false account of knowing, which would undermine humankind's highest achievements, if taken seriously. Polanyi claimed that the researchers are not independent in the face of their objects of study, for it is they who structure the framework of analysis, a framework particularly influenced by the culture of the researchers. He adds that the researcher cannot speak of accuracy, only plausibility.

Kuhn was an American who introduced the term "paradigm shift," now an English-language idiom. Kuhn claimed that scientific fields undergo periodic paradigm shifts rather than solely progressing in a linear and continuous way. The shifts open up new ways to understand what scientists would never have before considered valid. We cannot establish our notion of scientific truth, at any given moment, solely by objective criteria. Scientific truth is instead defined by the consensus of a given scientific community. Competing paradigms are irreconcilable accounts of reality. Hence - and this is profound - what we comprehend of science can never rely only on objectivity. We also take into account subjectivity, since researchers and participants use their conditioning and worldviews to draw their objective conclusions. Kuhn does not accept that science advances towards the truth. Science is not neutral. We cannot define science ontologically.

Conventionalism admits that anything considered relevant by the scientific community should be considered as a scientific object. Scientists are constantly negotiating their rules and criteria. There is a very intimate relationship between researchers and the objects they observe in a framework that they structure. Social and philosophical issues influence the accumulation of knowledge.

We recognize today that the natural sciences are complex, uncertain, and indeterminate; they exist in a chaotic universe. *A fortiori*, we can say that there is a conceptual indifferentiation between the different natural and human sciences. Scientists in all fields could explain their phenomena (e.g., group dynamics in a work environment) in relation to their beliefs, their provisions, the resources available to them, and the relationships between these same resources.

Cultural notions, expectations, and knowledge influence researchers, as we have partly seen in Chapter III. Defining science has always been difficult because it cannot claim to be based on a universally accepted methodology. I am rather on the side of the conventionalists who postulate that science does not follow rules and that it is the result of negotiations between scientists and their community (this is also true for workplace accident investigation teams). I am of the opinion that what a scientist examines and sees depends in large part on his/her expectations, experiences, and acquired knowledge. There is no universal method to define the veracity of a science. There is no universal method for an investigator or a coroner to determine the truth.

Accident investigations encompass technical research as well as research related to the economic, social, and political context. For example, we can say that a nuclear reactor leaked because the cooling system was lacking or that the negotiated working conditions caused fatigue in the workers who were monitoring the performance of the reactor. In the second case, investigators (researchers) can deliberately seek evidence to verify a hunch. Investigators are normally selective in their choice of assumptions. They claim that there is an absolute, that the theory informs the facts. However, they are making a conventionalist assumption. Absolute certainty does not exist when we draw causal conclusions from the sociological, political, economic, and psychological realms. All investigators are subjective when they observe human behaviour.

I understand that the theory I am putting forward in this book - that knowledge produced by investigators might be just another version of the truth - may not appear too virtuous to you. As Plato said about rhetoric, it may push you into cynicism. I am not saying that investigators do not produce valuable and useful knowledge. I am saying that truth is a valuation, a subjective judgment that varies. Investigators select - should select - the most valuable and serviceable truth, the one that has the most chance to improve safety. In order to do so, there needs to be a common understanding on the part of the investigation team that they are striving to find the best truth to improve safety. As can be said for philosophy, *"[t]he validity of a truth claim is nothing but the process in which it proves to be true; moreover, the validity endures only for as long as the process of factual proving-to-be-true continues - which explains the power and persuasiveness of a truth claim"* (Oehler, 2002).

Language permits humans to convey our theories beyond our own minds. We call this exosmotic. This makes possible the evolution of human reason, as well as the use of imagination and criticism in the search for truth. The difference between the growth of animal knowledge and of human knowledge is just this: criticism. To help me further explain my thoughts on the impossible search for the truth, for real proof, and for real science, I will dig further into the epistemology of science.

Karl Popper, an Austrian-British philosopher and professor who lived in the 20th century, believed that determinism was not a tenable theory and felt we had no reason to accept it. Nor did he accept the doctrine of free will. He did not believe in any theological arguments about divine grace orchestrating our daily lives or the evolution of the universe. As rationalists, if we accept indeterminism, we do not have to commit to the possibility of a superior entity overseeing us.

We generally categorize science as either being natural or social. This compartmentalization implicitly suggests that we teach scientific knowledge in these two streams differently. Even today, we may still hear the term "pure sciences," referring to the fields of research such as chemistry and physics. I studied both natural and social sciences. They are both impure sciences. Let me therefore start to fuse the two scientific fields by recalling the visions of natural science as conceived by the Inductivists and the Falsificationists.

According to Professor Alan Chalmers, a physicist with a primary interest in the philosophy of science, scientists first have vague ideas, develop concepts that they refine, and clarify until a theory emerges that they consider coherent and verifiable. They make their ideas by observation, induction. In his bestselling textbook *What Is This Thing Called Science?* (1987) Chalmers shows us that we cannot affirm the veracity of our science; we can only give it a probable value. Science is an accumulation of knowledge and the results acquired from searching for universal laws. Research proceeds through experimentation based on arbitrary rules. Popper asserts that there is no certainty or precision in science. Theories are not absolute but, once accepted by the community of scientists, they are determined to be accurate.

Popper rejected the classical inductivist view on the scientific method in favour of empirical falsification. According to Popper, we can never prove a theory in the empirical sciences, but we can falsify it. Theories are falsifiable (Popperian falsification). We make assumptions based on statements of observation that seem perfectly safe. However, as the history of science demonstrates, we criticize all hypotheses to the point of confirming their falsification. Theories are the closest we can get to the truth.

Paul Karl Feyerabend was an Austrian-born philosopher of science, famous for his purportedly anarchist view of science. He rejected the idea that there are universal methodological rules. He noted that, based on the history of science, we cannot reduce it to a few methodical rules. It would be detrimental to science to say that we can organize it according to fixed and universal rules. Chalmers says, in similar words, that it is always possible to find a situation in which science does not work. This is the case, in particular, for mathematics, where it has not yet been possible to find a universally accepted body (Kline, 1989). From the time of Aristotle, we developed mathematics to measure the physical world. In the 19th century, we began developing new branches of mathematics with more rigour and abstract foundations. Mathematics became the science that draws conclusions or, as Bertrand Russell said, generates "symbolic logic" (Russell, 1905). In all cases, mathematics makes hypothetical assertions, not categorical ones. Mathematics is not organized according to fixed and universal rules.

Kurt Friedrich Gödel was a logician, mathematician, and philosopher. He is considered, like Aristotle, to be one of the most significant logicians. He asserts that the notion of truth in mathematics is impossible. Morris Kline, a professor of mathematics, and a writer on the history, philosophy, and teaching of mathematics, deplored the conduct of mathematical research when one is not acquainted with the context needed to solve applied problems in sciences (Kline, 1989). Inventing pure mathematical problems without any purpose is akin to conducting mathematical research for just pure fun. Kline brings us to the idea that the physical world is not something we can feel. This is what mathematical theories say.

The social sciences analyze an individual's behaviour as that individual deploys his/her abilities. The social sciences also consider behaviour in the context of societies. The problem for the social science researcher is that the conditions in which the individual's behaviour is exercised change without the researcher being able to predict what they will be in advance. As a result, it becomes difficult to determine what is constant in the person's behaviour when the context is always changing. The result is that we can see the theory as incomplete and unstable. It is also the most compelling argument about the possibility and the impossibility of truth in the social sciences. Truth is volatile.

The goal of the natural sciences is to develop theories independently of context. This does not apply to the social sciences. While we need to have clarity about the object we are studying, this clarity is not possible when researching everyday life behaviour. There is a distinctive phenomenology between the natural and social sciences. They are two visions. To identify the goal of the social sciences, one needs to look into the epistemology, which I discuss in the section below. We can then also extrapolate that the same applies to the epistemology of accident investigation.

REALITY IN THE EYES OF THE BEHOLDER

As noted earlier, with respect to industrial accidents, the authority responsible for publishing the investigation report (accident investigation board or commission, or other independent government authorities such as health and safety boards) becomes the custodian of the truth. This authority cements the causes and contributing factors of the accident using the work of the investigation team. The following is a brief synopsis of the epistemology of the social sciences that is also salient to authorities that have a mandate to communicate their knowledge to the public.

To begin, the social science researcher must consider the values in play in order to describe this practical wisdom (also called *phronesis* as per Aristotle). Researchers have to assume that they can rationally explain and accept some values as universal. They must agree that they can interpret values and facts. Fundamentally, their challenge is to search to understand the struggle between workers in their social environment. This should be at the heart of their analysis. The social research question is, therefore, both Weberian (who governs?) and Nietzschean (what are the rational explanations that govern those who govern?). The social science researcher should try to approach and explain reality by considering values and struggle. Investigators, like social science researchers, must provide a context and qualify it by analyzing and illustrating individual actions in detail. They need to focus on things that may seem prima facie trivial.

Investigators need to always keep in mind that their work has to improve safety. Their quest for data is not about accumulating knowledge purely for the purpose of producing it. It is about producing practical wisdom pursuant to research and investigation. Investigators need to be interested in both understanding and explaining practical activities of individuals and society, without judging. Their object of study concretely exists. Both researchers and investigators must keep in mind how they will apply their findings in reality.

Researchers and investigators interpret social phenomena in relation to a process. They analyze intrinsically linked actors and their practices in relation to their social structures. The aim of researchers and investigators is to produce a practical dialogue and wisdom (praxis) in society. Researchers and investigation bodies are just one voice, the one that pragmatically interprets the subject studied. Alternatively, if one prefers, a voice that produces a *phronesis* search result. It is one voice, the official one, amongst a multitude of voices claiming to know the truth. In the area of workplace accidents, the focus is on understanding order and control in the daily relations between workers, employees, and governments (creating the rules and regulations of the work environment, including determining if ranges should have lights in the Arctic to help traffic adapt to climate change), and what causes this order and control to collapse.

Bent Flyvbjerg is a Danish economic geographer and professor of major program management at Oxford University. He has shown that competition between megaprojects promoters and their sponsors creates pressures at the organizational and political levels that result in the consistent overestimation of project benefits and the underestimation of project costs. One of his arguments to explain this is that the projects that look best on paper are the ones for which costs and benefits have been misrepresented the most. He also produced guidelines to explain social science research. He probably did not realize it in the moment, but he was producing transferable guidelines that can be applied to the field of accident investigation.

Flyvbjerg's guidelines are a method to research social sciences that is similar to what I discussed at the end of the last chapter. I looked at how to investigate accidents using accident theories *(Chapter II)* to explain error. First, we identify and describe the causes and effects that exist in the workplace. Second, we explain the conditions to which the worker is exposed. Then we look at formal and informal institutions and regulations that govern and administer practices.

Unfortunately, investigators tend to skim over the fourth step and skip the fifth step. In the fourth step, we look at the behaviour and perceptions of the actors involved. In the fifth step, we look at the historical, economic, political, social, and ideological contexts in which the elements manifested themselves or upon which they depended. Finally, and a key point, this social science methodology normally involves multidisciplinary experts, something often missing in accident investigations, but something that would greatly help investigators to become more aware of the role and the influences of context.

To explain the systemic nature of a particular experience, researchers need to use methods that consider all possible explanations. Researchers need to be exhaustive. Investigators make assumptions about reality or conceptualize this reality by making connections between facts that may appear disconnected from one another. The theories must link the postulate, the method used to develop the postulate, and the philosophy used to inform it. There is always ontology and epistemology. Social scientists, like investigators, validate their work based on the premise that there is a material and social world that is independent of individual consciousness, but which is intelligible and translatable in certain epistemological conditions.

Investigators, like philosophers, ask questions to understand social phenomena. They ask questions such as "How did this accident occur?" (A Hume-type question) and "What is true for the accident to occur?" (A Kant-type question.) They examine the nature of reality (ontology) and if their knowledge of this reality is possible (epistemology). They make assumptions about reality or conceptualize this reality by making connections between facts that may appear disconnected from one another. Investigators interpret the effects of social phenomena in relation to a process. They analyze actors and their practices in relation to the structures intrinsically linked with the actors. This is what philosophers and industrial accident specialists do: they try to discover reality (for accident investigators, discovering a reality that will improve safety). I emphasize here that it does not mean that investigators or philosophers succeed in discovering reality, or the truth. We are speaking about acquiring knowledge.

THE EMOTIONAL PURPOSE BEHIND THE STORY

Bruno Latour is a French philosopher whose work shakes the traditional foundation of how we acquire knowledge and determine what is real. Like many of his contemporaries, he has argued that scientific facts are a product of inquiry. He uses the term "networked" to posit that the inherent truth of facts is determined based on the strength of the network (institutions and practices) that produces the facts and renders them intelligible to the common person (Kofman, 2018). In essence, knowledge is the product of human procedures; scientists and investigators create it with their research.

There are two types of knowledge, rational and emotional. The latter creates the basis for the former and makes it possible. Logic itself shows that reason can only come after feelings. To search, to research, to investigate, we need to desire something; we need to desire understanding. This desired thing, the truth, is an absolute necessity, a basis for reasoning. We can only achieve our goal if we determine what we are searching to uncover. Unfortunately, in our modern world, we appear to have reversed our logic. Reasoning has taken the forefront. This may partly explain why we feel utterly distraught nowadays. Society is constantly searching for scientific truth - complete objectivity - to justify the actions it takes. We do not use shampoo because we want to feel and be clean; we use a particular brand of shampoo because it is "scientifically proven to give you richer, smoother, and stronger hair." We use a particular brand of toothpaste because "9 out of 10 dentists approve this clinically proven toothpaste," etc. We are constantly searching to justify why we do what we do.

There is no doubt that science has improved our lives. However, the trend toward rational intelligence is out of control; emotional intelligence is taking a backseat. We no longer ask ourselves what is good, but rather what is true, in the scientific sense of the term. Science, intrinsically, translates our daily lives in objective terms. There is nothing in nature that indicates the ethical value of things or people; ethics is subjective. The idea, therefore, is not to reject objectivity, but rather to re-establish it around the emotional desires of humankind. True wisdom should lead us to understand that we need *logos*, a dialogue between both types of knowledge.

Our search for the truth is merely a search for answers, logical explanations that may be devoid of the most fundamental unanswered question in today's investigation world: what is the emotional desire behind our work? The only purpose of investigation work should be to improve the lives of our fellow humans.

Searching and aiming to produce reports that are "right" - our view of what is "right" - is wasting taxpayers' dollars. Launching investigations merely because we signed an international convention that says what and when to investigate is a poor premise. Conventions were necessary to force various countries to create national investigation bodies. Today, we are seeing many reports that comply with the need to accumulate rational knowledge but are devoid of emotional knowledge.

The job of scientists and investigators is to produce knowledge, a most probable truth. Normally, they first establish the facts, and then use those facts to produce findings. Unfortunately, too often, investigators do this the wrong way. They start with pre-established beliefs. Then, they look for evidence to support them. This is also how we normally react when we want to find out causes and contributing factors for an occurrence at home, at work, or in our community. We want to know who is at fault.

We look for a culprit because we are sad, angry, or fearful. These feelings power us and are strong enough to create an obsession. We may not think clearly. We can rapidly draw false conclusions based on first impressions, preliminary evidence, hearsay, etc. We have a need to find a guilty party as we project ourselves into the scenario and want to play the innocent bystander. Innocence is very sweet. We use an incredible amount of time and energy focusing our brainpower to model causes and effects when dealing with social relationships. We spend a lot of effort to think about who has caused what to happen, to whom, and for what reason.

Humans are strongly motivated to seek causes for effects. This motivation is a factor in the prevalence of religions. When we lose or gain something of value, we seem to have a psychological need to place cause and effect, meaning, or context around it. Our history is paved with evidence that we have always had this compulsion to seek causes for effects. Primitive people practised various forms of sacrifice, including scapegoating (the term derives from the actual practice of releasing a goat into the wilderness to carry bad luck away), and whipping boys were used to suffer punishment deserved by another (the term derives from the Middle Ages when boys were beaten in the place of young nobles who had behaved badly). People will often rationalize away things they see but cannot explain, so they can feel like they have understood what happened. This helps them to better deal with it in the future. Placing blame on someone gives a similar illusion of having found the root of an issue; it becomes something you can understand and resolve by taking action, even if you may have found the wrong root or missed the actual root causes.

Early in human history, most people survived in small bands of humans and were dependent on each other. The bands usually consisted of up to 200 people (about as many people as you can comfortably know personally now). Our brains dedicated a lot of real estate to keep track of who did what to whom and when; this knowledge helped us find mates and avoid the "free-rider" problem of people mooching without contributing. People kicked out of society died, but people who mooched and got away with it survived. Hence, we have evolved with both an incentive to be selfish and an incentive to cooperate and contribute. Our brains are primed to notice who did what to whom, and to find ways to avoid being blamed for stuff we did not do (Harari, 2014). This can result in a blame game. We all do it, publicly or secretly.

Shakespeare, through the character of Queen Gertrude in Act IV of Hamlet, says that when a person feels guilty for something they have secretly done, they are likely to become extremely suspicious of others as a result. They may become hyper vigilant, out of fear of being exposed: "So full of artless jealousy is guilt, it spills itself in fearing to be spilt." People can often recognize this paranoid behaviour. This can result in guilty individuals exposing themselves through their very attempt at protecting themselves. And, if people do not expose themselves, then we feel compelled to search for a guilty party.

Humans want to know why and who is responsible for mishaps. How we proceed in our daily lives and how investigators proceed towards this endeavour may be very similar. The end to the means may, however, be very different. For accident investigators, they need to determine an emotional purpose that will circumscribe their findings. Then, they tell a compelling story, linking their analysis to facts. The result is an investigation report, a social construct. It is not about finding if someone is guilty of an infraction or punishable of an offence. The accident investigator is not bound by a burden of proof other than creating a defendable story.

The burden of proof is different when involving litigation. In criminal litigation, jurors have to decide, "beyond a reasonable doubt." In civil litigation, jurors decide on the balance of probability, which is "a pretty low standard" according to Scott Findlay, a professor at the University of Ottawa. Scientists and accident investigators use a different standard of proof when deciding if something causes cancer or what caused a disaster. To determine that A causes B, we need compelling evidence.

Truth is an elastic concept in civil litigation. Truth is also a concept, as we have seen, that may be debatable in science. Scientists can claim that there is never a satisfying ending to their work. Science is a permanently unfinished line of business. We accumulate knowledge. In contrast, investigators see their report as a finished product. They do not spend much time questioning the validity of their work. Investigators accumulate knowledge, but rarely ask themselves if they could have achieved different results - changes in the workers' environment - had they produced different findings. They rarely ask themselves the question "Should I have searched for a different truth?"

CLOSING ARGUMENTS

We recognize that the natural sciences are complex, uncertain, indeterminate, and that they exist in a chaotic universe. We covered the epistemology of the natural sciences and showed that it is difficult to claim that they are objective. In the same way, we cannot expect that knowledge acquired to explain rational planning in the workplace can be predictable, objective, or considered the absolute truth. Investigators need to consider that the knowledge they produce may only be capable of producing limited insights that do not go much below the surface of various phenomena.

Researchers in the social field, especially those in the field of industrial investigations, should capitalize on the idea that their field has an explanatory power, rather than a predictive power. Investigators do not use deductivism, which is based in a conception of science (e.g., positivism) and empirical realism. Investigators produce knowledge by using critical realism. Investigators use a philosophical and methodological framework to describe sociological phenomena. The ultimate goal of investigators is to illuminate and explain the causal mechanisms that give rise to social phenomena.

This metatheoretical framework raises practical questions about the activities and behaviours that take place in an industrial setting. Causal issues arise and questions are raised about the counterfactual and transfactual influences of governance structures, mechanisms, trends, and powers. Society needs to produce knowledge to explain workplace accidents and industrial disasters of all kinds. We need to pursue this endeavour. We also need to encourage debates on the knowledge that is produced and how investigation bodies construct their findings. This is a central proposal of the essay.

We have seen that there are similarities between the natural sciences and the social sciences, in particular the orthodox model of finding knowledge in the natural sciences and the so-called problem-solving model in the social sciences, which studies a stable object and accumulates knowledge that is definitive, cumulative, and transferable. For example, when calculating the gravitational force and reinterpreting it, a researcher creates his/her vision of reality according to immutable conditions. As Chalmers says, in similar words, "Scientific theories have an objective structure outside the minds of individual scientists and have properties that can or cannot be discovered and exhibited" (Chalmers, 1987). With industrial accidents, workers and their environments are constantly changing. Although there is an objective structure and we can define properties, we cannot talk about the static nature of work environments. Therefore, investigators, before finalizing their report, should review their conclusions with a view to maximize their value in space and time.

We should investigate to produce knowledge. This knowledge, a version of the truth, will be valid at the time of the accident investigation. It will also be valid for the *bona fide* investigation body that is determining the findings under a legitimized and transparent process. The knowledge accumulated during an investigation is a conception of reality.

Investigators need to ask themselves if they are clear on the desired outcome of their work. They should start by laying down the emotional knowledge they want to acquire. This would ensure that they are achieving the best bang for their buck - that is, the best chance of improving safety.

Of course, this may be a moot point if the authority responsible for publishing the investigation team's work modifies the content of the report to reflect their own understanding of how failure happened. It is also the responsibility of the publishing authority to understand the emotional purpose behind the investigation before they decide what truth needs to be conveyed to the public.

V

The Uncomfortable Truth
And Why We Avoid It

> › *Communicating knowledge*
> › *Lying and deceiving come naturally*
> › *Motivated, skeptical, biased, segmented… the public*
> › *Perception vs. reality - the eternal struggle*
> › *Trust is a rare commodity*

It is 20 April 2010, in the Gulf of Mexico. Staff on the oil platform *Deepwater Horizon* are carrying out their duties, sleeping, eating, or taking a break on this seemingly uneventful day. Sam, Norm, and Alex are part of the on-watch team. They conduct checks to ensure that they properly sealed the borehole, a narrow vertical shaft pierced into the seabed that is used to extract oil. Sam looks at Norm and says, "I told you guys that we pumped sufficient cement yesterday." Pumping cement is a standard procedure intended to prevent leaks. The main work for everyone these past days had been finalizing the drilling of an exploratory well at Macondo, some 70 kilometres off the U.S. coast.

Then, the unthinkable occurs. A geyser of seawater erupts onto the rig, shooting 240 feet (73 metres) high. Shortly afterwards, Sam, Norm, and Alex witness the eruption of a slushy combination of drilling mud, methane gas, and water. Norm, with Sam's help, attempts to activate the blowout preventer, a valve that, once closed, is able to cope with extreme erratic pressures and uncontrolled flow emanating from the well. The preventer uses the principle of a wedge to seal the bore and prevent oil from escaping. Both men apply force on the wheel-like handles in an attempt to activate the valve, but they cannot overcome the high pressure applied against the mechanism. Their efforts fail. Unbeknownst to them, the pipeline going through the preventer was slightly bent, meaning the valve couldn't perform as designed.

There is a last resort when it comes to preventing an oil spill: activating the blind shear ram, a device designed to cut the pipe in the well. Alex was quick to try to get the system to work. He knew that the rams needed to move down so that steel blades would shear the pipe and seals. He hoped for the pipe to shear and the ram to seal the bore. This also failed.

The gas component of the slushy material (drilling mud, methane gas, and water) transitioned into a fully gaseous state that then ignited in a series of explosions and a firestorm. Eleven rig workers died, including Sam, Norm, and Alex. The remaining 115 workers on the rig were evacuated, many were injured; all were airlifted. The *Deepwater Horizon* sank on 22 April 2010, two days later. The remains of the rig were found resting on the seafloor in a location approximately 5,000 feet (1,500 metres) deep and about 1,300 feet (400 metres) northwest of the well. The Macondo blowout led to the largest marine oil spill in the history of the petroleum industry.

A massive response ensued to protect the environment from the spreading oil (it is estimated that a total of five million barrels had been released in the environment by the time the well was sealed). There was extensive damage to marine and wildlife habitats, as well as the fishing and tourism industries. The beaches of Louisiana required cleaning; workers removed several thousand tons of oily material. Oil and a dispersant mixture were found embedded in the sand as far away as the Florida Panhandle and Tampa Bay. Marine life continued to die long after the blowout.

Day after day, viewers around the world were glued to their TV screens, learning about several failed efforts to contain the flow. This very sad story made headlines for weeks. Numerous private and public investigations explored the causes of the explosion and the record-setting spill. The reports pointed to defective cement on the well, faulting mostly the owner, but also the rig operator and the contractor. Blame went to the company and its partners for a series of cost-cutting decisions and an inadequate safety system. Various investigations concluded that the spill resulted from systemic root causes.

So far, we have covered how disasters happen, but we have not spent much time discussing the communications that happen during the unfolding of a disaster or immediately following one. We have not yet covered how we communicate safety messages at the time we publish investigation reports.

To help us prepare to release a report publicly, including preparing for a press conference, we analyze the media coverage of the accident or disaster. We generally get a good idea what the press may be asking when we are on the hot seat immediately following an accident, at the scene, or being interviewed live on the phone or in front of a remote camera. The media challenges us, they ask questions that the public wants answered. We strive to understand the concerns of the workers and the public. We start this research from the onset of the disaster.

* * *

THE INVESTIGATOR'S MAZE

We are now at the last maze. I continue to present questions specifically to the accident that is introduced and are relevant to the theory studied in each chapter, providing some insight into the inquisitive mind of an accident investigator.

In the last chapter, we pursued and completed the quest to come up with a story, the knowledge to improve safety and protect the environment. The last phase of an investigation, your last goal, is to communicate the safety messages to the companies, various actors (workers), witnesses, and the public.

While communicating can take different forms and use different media platforms, how you prepare to do this will always entail sketching out or developing a formal communications plan. It is wise to start this endeavour by laying out a series of questions relevant to the accident.

· What are the impacts on people and the environment?

· Is the public emotionally charged?

· Is the public blaming someone or an organization?

· Will I be perceived as an honest broker?

· How did spokespeople handle the crisis?

* * *

THE LAST STEP, LAST CHALLENGE... COMMUNICATING

Communicating the truth is the most difficult and critical part of an investigation. Writing and communicating the findings of an investigation is, in many ways, a game of deception, something we all do at work, at home, and in our everyday social encounters, whether we recognize it or not. I will demonstrate in this chapter how we do it and explain why we do it. Communicating truth requires two main abilities and one main personal value. An individual needs highly intuitive and discursive thinking capacities. One also needs strong altruistic values, something that is difficult for most people to possess since Homo sapiens are social animals and self-centred by nature. However, to conduct an investigation and to ensure the truth uncovered can positively influence society, an investigator needs these three qualities.

Spokespeople, including investigators in charge, have a daunting task of communicating with the public through the media during an emergency and providing the findings of an investigation following an often-controversial event. I have experienced this firsthand both as the head of investigations and as on-scene commander for major marine environmental accidents. I have learned that the training provided to spokespeople fails to teach them two fundamental concepts about risk communication. The first is that there is a flaw in the message we convey because we are limited to providing our perspective, our knowledge. There exists other valid knowledge, other truths, held by the people to whom we communicate. The second is that the training is based on selling evidence-based data to a majority of the population that is skeptical about you and your message. To add to this challenge, these folks are generally the ones that need to change their ways if we want to improve safety.

You may remember British Petroleum's (BP) CEO Tony Hayward. He is the executive who came out publicly on May 30, 2010, after the disastrous *Deepwater Horizon* spill, to deliver a poorly prepared statement: *"I'm sorry. We're sorry for the massive disruption it has caused their lives. And there is no one who wants this over more than I do. I'd like my life back."* He somewhat got his life back - he lost his job after he apologized for his apology. On Facebook, he wrote: *"I made a hurtful and thoughtless comment on Sunday when I said that I wanted my life back. When I read that recently, I was appalled. I apologize, especially to the families of the 11 men who lost their lives in this tragic accident."* Hayward's stumble would not be the only public relations mishap from BP. If you want to communicate how you are managing a crisis or you want to communicate your version of the events - your truth - just remember that the story is not about you. Being altruistic is an important quality for an investigator and, especially, a spokesperson.

This chapter will discuss communicating accidents and disasters to the public. Those who specialize in being public spokespeople learn part of their trade, communicating during a crisis, from watching the best and the worst. They also, like most investigators, learn how to communicate findings from standard training provided to public spokespeople such as politicians and CEOs. The training skims over the concepts of deceit, lying, and hiding the truth, without considering these concepts in depth. The trainers do not use the terms *deceit*, *lying*, or *the truth*. The trainers mainly focus on the *bona fide* message you want to deliver. The training talks about facts, about communicating acquired knowledge. I try to cover ground here that does not exist in standard communication training for investigators.

I believe that spokespeople first need to understand that their mission is to sell debatable knowledge. They first need to understand how people generally communicate their knowledge. The training rarely considers the emotions of the public. The training does not consider how people develop their perceptions of you. You, the spokesperson, see yourself as an honest and credible broker of information. However, many may see you in another light, especially if you are presenting debatable findings.

There are three parts in this chapter. I first provide knowledge on lying and deceiving, something we all do that may taint the way we look at people who deliver a public message. In the second part, you will learn that your audience can be motivated, skeptical, biased, and how a prominent risk communicator suggests you segment the public in order to understand how to adapt your message. This is key if you want to instill change, improve safety. Finally, I explain the concept of trust and provide some insight into the public's perception of spokespeople.

PERCEPTION IS REALITY... NO, REALLY

We saw in the previous chapter that accident investigators accumulate knowledge in the form of findings. How investigators communicate requires that they first agree that their knowledge is debatable. Evidence-based science, like investigation reports into accidents, is a version of knowledge put together by an individual or a group using their process and evidence. Keep this in mind. Telling the story about a mechanical failure and limiting our finding to the physical evidence is a relatively easy task. You will not face much resistance; selling your message will be a walk in the park.

However, when you straddle the line of human conflict and social interactions, or comment on how work-is-done versus how work-was-imagined, you are communicating a point of view, your position. Investigating for human factors means producing knowledge that humans fail. People do not like to be told they fail. Brace yourself for a bumpy ride. Communicating about social, political, and economical risks in the workplace is a dodgy task.

Lying is an easy concept to grasp. Nevertheless, I will cover this in detail. Before I move on to the science of lying and deceiving, let me use an example to introduce the latter so you better understand how this fits with telling your story to the public. It will help you understand how one can purposely or involuntarily communicate a deceitful message.

The Hague III Convention on the Opening of the Hostilities of October 18, 1907, clearly establishes the requirement for a declaration of war: *"Hostilities should not commence without previous warning."* You should wait to open hostilities until you inform the aggressor in *"the form of either a reasoned declaration of war or an ultimatum with conditional declaration of war."*

Japan attacked Pearl Harbor on December 7, 1942, before having delivered a declaration of war. Japan disputes this. The attack on Pearl Harbor was not a "sneak" attack upon a nation at peace. There was a lawful declaration of war. I do not want to go into a historical analysis, but rather use this example to show that if you want to deceive, you can do many things and claim that you are the custodian of the truth. It is clear in this infamous saga and dramatic killing of Americans that a telegram from Japan to the U.S. required decoding and translating into English. Japan could have timed this telegram to ensure that the notification would not arrive before the attack.

Japan had made its decision to go to war with the U.S. several months earlier. The Imperial Japanese navy trained and made its way towards U.S. territory well before the Japanese government sent the telegram asserting that it considered it was *"impossible to reach an agreement through further negotiations."* Finally, officials in the Japanese government were aware that the telegram was not a proper declaration of war. In fact, the Foreign Ministry had drafted a formal declaration of war that it never sent to the U.S. The document remained in the Foreign Ministry's Historical Archive until it was unearthed in 1997 by Professor R.J. Butow at the University of Washington. In short, if you want to avoid the truth, there are many ways you can do so.

Nowadays, there always seems to be someone calling out false news. There are also political myths, such as the myth that the U.S. government was behind the September 11 attacks. Myths share a link with reality but are interpreted with an ideological bias. Dismantling myths can be a difficult and disputable exercise as you try to consider one interpretation in opposition to another. You also have to consider that an interpretation is never totally objective, which is especially important to know with today's rise of populism in western societies.

Creating myths can be easy. On the night of 2 December 1984, and into the early morning hours of the next day, more than 500,000 people were exposed to methyl isocyanate gas (MIC) at the Union Carbide India Limited (UCIL) pesticide plant in Bhopal, India. The highly toxic substance made its way into and around the shantytowns located near the plant. The local government confirmed a total of 3,787 deaths related to the gas release. Other estimates state that 8,000 died within two weeks and another 8,000 or more died subsequently from gas-related diseases. What happened? The cause of this largest industrial disaster is still under debate.

The Indian government and local activists claim that slack management and deferred maintenance resulted in the back flow of water into an MIC tank. This triggered the disaster. Union Carbide Corporation (UCC) agrees that water entered the tanks, but through an act of sabotage. Same result and same error, but the guilty party is different. One story appears as the truth, the other may appear as a myth or a lie.

To help you investigate and communicate your knowledge, your version of the truth, you will want to know how humans perceive and communicate reality. Research conducted by Paul Ekman and Maureen O'Sullivan concluded that it is difficult to detect deceit. In fact, during their 20 years of research, Ekman and O'Sullivan found that the accuracy of people's ability to determine if a subject was lying rarely exceeded 60 percent. You can therefore imagine how difficult it may be for investigators to determine what is true or false when they conduct interviews with a suspect, a person involved in an accident, or a witness.

Not only is it hard to detect deceit, but investigators also have to remember that humans can involuntarily omit relevant information and thus deceive unintentionally. According to Daniel Goleman in his book *Vital Lies, Simple Truths* (1996), the mind can focus on what is salient and ignore some essential components of a task. A new social reality can then be created that omits some critical information. This thesis centres on our ability to create a reality that prevents us from experiencing anxiety.

For his part, Jeffrey Pfeiffer reports in his book *Leadership BS* (2015) that, based on large literature review, the memory plays tricks and frequently makes recall unreliable for eyewitness accounts of accidents or crimes. Reality may differ for different eyewitnesses based on a construed opinion or a different perception. Police officers know that witnesses will report hearing different numbers of shots after a shooting. Four witnesses may have four different versions of what they witnessed. Each has their own perception of the reality. And the truth may even be something entirely different.

People perceive messages and see things according to their own perspective. In day-to-day conflict with co-workers, friends, or spouses, differing perceptions are often the genesis of the fight. Who is right and who is wrong may be based on shared or unshared values. Investigators need to know the genesis of conflict in the workplace; they also need to know that their audience may perceive things differently when they are being presented facts by a government or industry spokesperson. One must always doubt. This is a cardinal virtue which, drawing its origins from the skeptical tradition, prefers the suspension of judgment to the favour of universal certainties. As Philip Roth wrote in *American Pastoral*:

> *The fact remains that getting people right is not what living is all about anyway. It's getting them wrong that is living, getting them wrong and wrong and wrong and then, on careful reconsideration, getting them wrong again. That's how we know we're alive: we're wrong. Maybe the best thing would be to forget being right or wrong about people and just go along for the ride. But if you can do that - well, lucky you.*

Not only must we keep in mind that individual perceptions may differ wildly, but we also must remember that humans possess the drive to deceive. In fact, this drive may be a reason for why human beings are intelligent. We all tell lies, several times a day, and remain unflustered about our own attitudes. Yet, all of us are offended to learn, even from our closest friend or family members, that we were lied to. Avoiding the truth is a necessity to function in society. Our engrained culture of deception is a necessity for our survival.

When people are caught unprepared in the act of trying to deceive, their minds become overwhelmed. They cannot think properly. Humans are liars. We all lie, and we do so many times each day. We are all guilty of the standard little lies: "I am fine, thank you," or "What a lovely haircut you have." Why do we fib or stretch the truth? To what extent is this trait an impediment to functioning in society? Alternatively, is it an absolute necessity to lie in order to maintain harmony? We may also lie if we think our reputation is at stake.

We all tell white lies. Sometimes we tell people that the "traffic was terrible coming to work," "the food is delicious," and "we love your gift," when, in fact, these things are not the truth at all. While telling these small untruths is not necessarily the right thing to do, it is understandable and normal that we do it.

We acquired our linguistic skills over 70,000 years ago. We developed these skills in order to gossip, find out who could be trusted, and develop tighter cooperation between bands. Gossiping is something we all do frequently. It may well be the main reason humans acquired the ability to talk. We are, after all, social animals, as Aristotle claimed. We survive and reproduce because of our ability to cooperate with others. We started acquiring linguistic skills because it was important for us to know information about those around us, like which tribe hates which tribe, who is trading with whom, which are the trustworthy tribes, which are not, etc. We continue to gossip today; it is, in fact, our main social goal in life (Harari, 2014). Gossiping often straddles the line between tittle-tattle and speaking the truth.

We are experts at inventing stories. We collaborate with each other to create fiction. We knit together great myths, such as biblical stories. After the agriculture revolution, our ancestors started to invent stories about gods and their lands. These stories provided important social links. We were part of the group. We felt a sense of belonging. Today, we continue on in the same way; we associate together, we socialize to tell stories, share myths. We educate our children about the fundamental stories that shape our human existence and remind them of the imagined order incorporated into just about everything; we create a connection with the idea of inventing stories. The tapestry of life is woven together because of our rich collective imagination, and we imagine the order that organizes our lives (Harari, 2014). Just think about paintings, songs, dramas, hairstyles, tattoos, etiquette, propaganda, sporting rules, etc. It is in our genes to invent, inventing often involves deceiving, or stretching the truth - lying.

Oftentimes, we invent a truth, and then we aim to change the consciousness of our audience and convince them to believe it. For the change to succeed, we need to rally the entire organization behind our truth. This is also true for ideological movements and political parties. Cult leaders know that their challenge is to get strangers to accept their imagined order, their myths. Creating a subjective reality such as an investigation report - a social construct - is not all that different from trying to sell a gospel. We are not lying and we are not deceiving. We truly think we are selling the truth when we communicate the results of an investigation. We are doing what we are programmed to do: tell a story that we have created.

As humans, we lie so often that we expect it; we are unflustered when we say we are having a good day while we feel miserable inside. We may not like the haircut someone just got, but most of us will find a way to escape telling the truth, fibbing our way out of a difficult position that would embarrass a friend or a colleague. This is normal practice for everyone, regardless of cultural background. Moreover, we lie in order to deceive others or embellish ourselves, recasting situations so we come out smelling rosy, gaining respect and affection. This is human nature. Thomas Hobbes, one of the founders of modern political philosophy, puts a different spin on why we act the way we do. For him, we are masking our true selves to ensure social acceptance to survive. He proposes that humans are cooperative out of self-interest, and that political communities are based upon a social contract. Put another way, leading psychologists in the field say we present an edited and packaged version of ourselves to each other.

A study conducted by Bella M. DePaulo et al. in 1996 revealed that a sample of college students would lie, on average, once for every three social interactions, while a sample of participants from the community would lie once for every five social interactions. The study found that all people lie. The study also found, somewhat reassuringly, that we tell lies more for psychological reasons than for personal gain.

Megan Garber, in *The Atlantic* magazine, reports that, on average, we lie 1.65 times a day. You will not be surprised to learn that it has also been found that 81 percent of online daters exaggerate their attributes on their profiles. Following a survey conducted by *Sales and Marketing Management* magazine, Erin Strout reports that 316 sales and marketing executives stated that their representatives had lied 45 percent of the time about promised delivery dates. Some of us are better at speaking the truth and some of us are professionals at deceiving. Life is sprinkled with lies. We know it. We do it. So, we also expect others to do it, no matter who they are, what the situation is, and what the story is about.

Dan Ariely, a professor of behavioural economics and psychology at Duke University, has explored reasons for why we lie to each other and ourselves. He explains that there are many reasons for our dishonesty. First, we need motivation to see reality in a certain way. For example, when we determine that a referee has made a bad call against our hockey team, we are motivated to see the action unfolding as we hoped it had: "The referee made the wrong decision; the goal was good." Second, we need the rules to be flexible if we are going to lie and be credible. Without flexibility, your lie cannot make sense. "I did not see Bobby taking the last cookie," Ryan may reply to his mother after she asks if he took the last cookie. Ryan did not see his brother taking the cookies. He only participated in eating them. True, Ryan did not see Bobby, but he helped destroy part of the evidence. He is truthful to his mother, even though he knows she just really wants to know who took the last cookie.

Lastly, there needs to be a grey zone in order for one to rationalize one's own dishonesty. It was a rainy day in Montreal. I was wearing a business suit, and I was on my way to an important meeting. I did not have an umbrella, and I jaywalked in order to reach my destination faster and escape the rain. As I crossed the street, another man followed me. A cop on the beat saw us both and walked over to meet us as we arrived on the other side of the street. I knew I was going to get a ticket. The officer asked us why we would put our lives in danger by jaywalking. The rain continued to drip down on our increasingly sodden suits. The cop was dry in his rain gear. My partner in crime responded first and said, "I have no reason to put my life in danger." The cop replied, "Good answer" and turned to me. Dripping wet and knowing that the cop knew I had crossed to avoid having to continue ruining my suit, I answered: "Same here, Officer, I have no reason." I did not mind lying.

It was obvious to anyone that we wanted to risk our lives (not really, the street was clear of cars) to get to the other side of the road quickly. I do not know if the cop expected that I would lie or if he just wanted to show us his power. The cop knew we had a reason for jaywalking. Each of us did have a reason. But he gave me the grey zone necessary for me to justify my lie to myself. I could have told the truth - that I wanted to escape the rain and get to my destination quickly. But I purposely lied, saying that I did not have a reason, rationalizing my dishonesty to myself by saving $60 and getting the okay to get going on my way again.

As George Orwell said, *"In an age of universal deceit, telling the truth is a revolutionary act."* Or, as Mark Twain said, *"Truth is such a precious commodity, it should be used sparingly."* We hide and disguise the truth because the truth can evoke emotions that we do not want to face; it can make us feel uncomfortable, ashamed, angry, hurt, fearful, or worse. We also play around with feelings and emotions to present reality, or one's perception of reality - crying while telling a story can make us more credible; we play with the feelings of our interlocutor. We have all tried, at one time or another, to present reality differently from how it actually was - to revise it for our own purposes. At one time or another, we are in denial; the truth seems far-fetched. At other times, we find ways to conceal our true feelings; we find ways to deceive. Deception is, in fact, vital to our survival and to maintaining civility in society. Put in the words of Professor Richard Sennett: *"In practising social civility, you keep silent about things you know clearly but which you should not and do not say."* (Kahn-Harris, 2018)

We recognize that denial can be harmful. However, it is a way for us to respond to the challenge of living with other people. Denial should not be confused with denialism, which is rooted in a different tendency of some, not all, human beings. Denialism can be a direct assault on facts or a convenient reaction to modern science. For example, for those wishing to believe the biblical account of creation literally, it is convenient to reject the Darwin evolution theory. Denial and denialism, however, both have a similar root: our vulnerability to denial. As the sociologist Keith Kahn-Harris (2018) says, *"To be in denial is to know at some level. To be a denialist is to never have to know at all."*

When we know or suspect that someone is lying to us, our initial reactions are typically anger and judgment. We get upset and immediately make up our mind about the character of the individual in question. Most investigators, when acting in the role of a spokesperson, consider themselves to be honest brokers of information. However, they need to remember that when they communicate their knowledge about social, political, or economic phenomena related to an accident, many may think that they are being deceived, especially those who do not share the opinion espoused by the investigator.

(MY) TRUTH WILL SET YOU FREE

Ted Cruz, a Texas senator, is certain that global warming stopped as the new millennium was on the horizon. You can witness this yourself if you watch the Senate hearing on the Commerce, Science, and Transportation Subcommittee of December 2015. Cruz was the chair, and claimed that satellite data or, as he says,

"The science behind claims of global warming" shows that *"there has been no significant global warming for the past 18 years."* He then asked retired Rear Admiral David Titley about the *"pause in global temperatures."* Admiral Titley, a former chief oceanographer and navigator of the U.S. Navy, is now a meteorology professor at Penn State. He pointed to his own chart that used data from thermometers on the earth's surface. It was clear to anyone viewing the chart at the Senate Committee - and to me - that more than a century's worth of temperature data shows an unmistakable warming trend. *"I'm just a simple sailor,"* said Titley, *"but it's hard for me to see the pause on that chart. So I think the pause has kind of come and gone."*

Cruz rebutted that his own chart focused on data from satellites. Titley shot back, stating that satellite measurements have a number of significant problems - the reading of satellite imagery should be done with caution given that there is a degree of uncertainty compared to land-based thermometers. Satellites do not make direct measurements of temperature, but instead pick up microwaves from oxygen molecules in the atmosphere that vary with temperature. Satellites measure temperatures in the atmosphere, high above the earth's surface. The temperature readings can be drastically affected by fluctuations in a satellite's orbit, as well as altitude and calibrations to its microwave-sensing equipment.

The chart that Cruz uses shows the lower troposphere, which is about six miles above the earth's surface. While this data is an important piece of the climate and weather system, it does not tell the whole story. In addition, of course, to support the data on the veracity of climate change, we can use other less disputable data. Surface temperatures on land and in the oceans are increasing; sea ice is decreasing; glaciers are shrinking; oceans are rising, etc. However, none of this seems to really matter for the climate change deniers and for Cruz.

Like Admiral Titley, I am just a simple sailor, but I also have an opinion on what the better truth may be with respect to climate change. There are at least two opinions, whether the climate is changing, or it is not. We are preoccupied with debating the facts, which is sort of a way of life for us all. The author Thomas E.

Ricks, referring to King, the hero of George Orwell's novel 1984, writes: *"King was arguing that in a world based on facts, in which the individual has the right to perceive and decide those facts on his or her own, the state must earn the allegiance of its citizens. When it fails to live up to its rhetoric, it begins to forfeit that loyalty. This is a thought at once profoundly revolutionary and very American."* (Ricks, 2017)

Individuals estimate the probability that a hypothesis is true by assigning likelihood to it. However, most people are poor at assessing likelihood because they process information and form their beliefs in a biased manner. Specialists in the fields of psychology, political science, and communications sometimes refer to this concept as motivated reasoning. The concept was formulated in the second half of the 20th century and essentially posits that people are skeptical about information that does not fit their prior understanding of an issue. Individuals tend to retrieve thoughts and reasoning that align with their prior attitudes. When confronted with new knowledge, they process and reason with either positive or negative feelings. They select and evaluate knowledge more positively when it supports previously held beliefs and attitudes. They are less likely to accept and change their beliefs when faced with information that contradicts their thinking. Motivating people to process information that generates negative feelings takes time and effort.

We perceive risk according to our values, our cultural views that the anthropologist Mary Douglas classifies along two dimensions, "group" and "grid." Respectively, you are more likely to be an individualist versus a communitarian or a hierarchist versus an egalitarian. We situate ourselves relative to the two-end scale. You therefore have four quadrants that match the way people around the world generally view risk: individualist-hierarchist; communitarian-hierarchist; communitarian-egalitarian; and, individualist-egalitarian. Douglas calls this thinking, "The cultural theory of risk.

Cruz would be an individualist-hierarchist, while Titley would be a communitarian-egalitarian. Cruz does not see climate change as a high risk, while Titley does. Put another way, the senator sees climate change as a low risk (individualist-hierarchist) while the admiral sees it as a high risk (communitarian-egalitarian)(See figure 4).

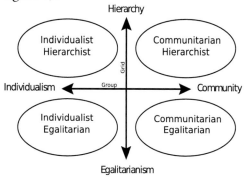

Fig. 4   After Douglas, Wildavsky, Flynn, Slovic, Kahan, etc.

You and I tend to accept or reject behaviour and ideas depending on where we find ourselves in the debate, where we determine what is good and honourable for society. We look for science that supports our cultural disposition, our tendency to perceive risks and related facts in relation to personal values. Our beliefs on controversial issues match the beliefs of peers and others, including scientists that believe in similar values. You and I consider information to be true - the truth - according to our cultural predisposition. The more we learn, the more polarized we become.

Professor Dan Kahan, from Yale Law School, is a researcher for the Cultural Cognition Project (CCP), a *"group of scholars interested in studying how cultural values shape public risk perceptions and related policy beliefs."* He says that *"people fit their perceptions of risk and related facts to their group commitments."* He calls this cultural cognition. Basically, in a debate, you are most likely to occupy the side - the side of truth - that your peers occupy. (Kahan, 2013)

The CCP conducted a study in which they measured subjects' values and divided them into individual-hierarchists and communitarian-egalitarianists. Subjects were presented a photo of a scientist and a mock CV. They were asked to determine, based on the photo and the mock CV if the scientist was an expert on a risk issue. The photo of the low-risk scientist was a serious-looking, clean-cut, shaved man in a suit, while the high-risk scientist was a smiling, bald, bearded man wearing a loose shirt. The subjects were divided in two groups and were shown different excerpts of the scientists' writing.

One group saw the scientist defend a low-risk position on climate change (also the position taken by Cruz), while the other subjects were shown the scientist defending the high-risk position (also the position taken by Titley). Individualist-hierarchists were highly likely to rate the scientist defending the low-risk position as an expert, while the communitarian-egalitarians were highly unlikely to rate the scientist defending the low risk position as an expert. The subjects' assessments would also be similar for other issues. The subjects credited or discredited the scientists' expertise according to their cultural predispositions. In other words, the subjects showed biased assimilation.

We all have various biases when we are trying to establish who is telling us fiction and who is telling the truth. We might judge a person based on appearance, manner of speaking, or the way they structure their argument. We tend to get very upset when we are telling a story, or a truth and our audience mocks us or dismisses our version. We want to project an image of ourselves as credible and correct. So do our peers and audience. We all tend to hold fast to our familiar beliefs even when confronted with new, contradicting knowledge.

Fortunately, few investigation findings are identity defining. The delivery of a message related to technical findings is easier than a message about social or policy issues related to culture or engrained habits, for example. Nevertheless, people have biases that are deep-seated in our cognitive architecture which may add a layer of complication to your communication plan.

KNOW YOUR AUDIENCE

Humans are capable of changing their behaviour and modifying their deficient practices. However, it is a daunting task for a spokesperson to install a behavioural change. Social change is slow. Consider how much time it took to convince people to wear ski helmets, put winter tires on their vehicles, or quit smoking. The change that came about as a result of these campaigns was painstaking and costly. To provoke safety-related change, spokespeople try to sell data, show the consequences of bad habits, and explain their knowledge about the conditions and underlying factors that lead to accidents.

Inducing change remains a challenge even when communicating to highly literate and educated people: hospitals around the world have difficulties ensuring surgeons wash their hands before they operate. Bringing about change requires long years of intervention and reinforcement. Often, change is only possible if workers are coerced into it.

We need to know where the audience stands on an issue if we are going to be successful in communicating a difficult message. You cannot just jump onto the stage with a prepared presentation that omits the most crucial element of communicating: understanding your audience. People shape their opinions based on their values and local circumstances (e.g., living in a tourist area where an environmental spill may hamper business opportunities). Truth is not universal; it can have a regional and even micro-regional flavour. Also, as we have seen, people are subject to motivated reasoning.

Most spokespeople believe that they can eventually sell their knowledge through communicating ever more data and through incorporating their knowledge into public education. Just ask anyone at your office or at your next cocktail gathering about how you can convince people to adopt a new behaviour. You probably will get the standard answer: "Show them the data backed by good science. Educate people." Wrong.

Professor Peter Sandman, a prominent expert in risk communication, says that the public is generally made up of five types of people. First, there are the radicals; they firmly believe their own truth. This group includes irrationalists and denialists (e.g., creationists, anti-vaxxers, and flat-earthers). Political scientists have shown that irrational people, especially those who are highly educated, may dig their heels in deeper when faced with a fact - a truth - that contradicts their own thinking.

"Simply telling people they are ignorant has failed. We need a better way to communicate," writes Ellie Mae O'Hagan, a freelance journalist writing for the Guardian. I remember when, almost 20 years ago, my daughters reached the age for the measles vaccination. A neighbour told me that his daughter had contracted diabetes after her measles vaccination; he was politely discouraging me from going ahead with my plan to have my daughters vaccinated. I double-checked the data that I had available and found that there were risks, but the overwhelming benefits outweighed the dangers.

Just in the last year, cases of measles have increased by 50 percent. Many credit this increase to a study conducted by a disgraced former doctor who asserted that there was a link between the vaccine and autism. You may think you can change the minds of these anti-vaxxer parents by going to their social media sites and trying to convince them that they are wrong. But you are wrong. Doing so has the exact opposite effect. You become part of the conspiracy. The University of Edinburgh conducted research using a bogus study and determined that using myth-busting techniques increased participants' belief in the bogus study. They noted that, *"Misinformation lingers in memory"* (O'Hagan, 2019).

Repeating a conspiracy theory, even if to debunk it, reminds people that the theory exists, lodging it in their consciousness. Human beings are not fact-processing machines. If you continue sending them facts that contradict their opinions, they will likely become offended, angry, and/or defensive, because you are telling them they cannot see the world in the same way you do. When facts challenge their opinions, people quickly become irritated, especially when it comes to the less savvy people that fill the Internet forums. They dig in their heels and defend their opinion, regardless of how irrational it may be.

Radicals, irrationalists, and denialists rarely change their opinions. They will always claim to be the custodians of the truth, the only truth. These folks should not be confused with the second of the five groups, those who are indifferent. This group does not generally vote; they do not care. They will not engage unless you entertain them. This group consists of many who need to change their habits if safety is going to be improved. A common attitude among this group is "Grandpa and Dad did things the same way, and even if they died doing it, I am going to continue doing the same thing." You need to entertain them, not just play on their emotions. They need to leave the discussion having enjoyed themselves.

The third group is very open. They listen and are searching to make up their minds. You can provide your story, your truth. They are eager to learn. The fourth group requires a smooth touch. They have an opinion and have already heard yours - from you or someone else. They participate somewhat actively in the debate. They came to the discussion intending not to change their minds. For this group, you must start your approach by explaining to them that their position is a valid one. You must show them why they have the opinion they have: society believed in A, just like you do because of B. You must show them that it is okay for them to have the opinion they have. Then, you can explain that society now has a new set of rules, or has discovered a new way of doing things that is more efficient, more environmentally friendly, etc.

You first go to their side and show them that you were also one of them until you saw the light. This technique does not necessarily mean that you will succeed in getting them to believe your truth, but it is an option that you should consider including in your toolbox. You validate their beliefs, and then you show them the data, testimonials, and facts. You take them on a trip in your own area of belief, but only after you have confirmed that their area of belief is valid - was valid.

The last group is ambivalent. They have more than one opinion and participate somewhat in the debate. If you want to succeed in getting an ambivalent audience to believe your truth, you need to understand their ambivalence. After that, you can determine whether you might be able to move them towards your position. For example, let us assume that you are a risk communicator, someone exchanging *"real-time information, advice and options between experts and people facing threats to their health, environmental or social well-being."* (WHO, 2019.) You have a public meeting with citizens who have come to hear you talk about the impacts of building a new pipeline destined to transport heavy crude oil. Let us say you are a spokesperson for the newly acquired Canadian federal government pipeline that goes from Alberta to the shore of the Pacific Ocean in British Columbia. The chances of a major disaster occurring, such as the pipeline spilling hundreds of thousands of tons of nasty tar sands oil into the pristine waters of Burnaby, BC, is both horrible and unlikely. Many citizens are on the fence; they do not know if they should believe whether a major disaster is about to happen or whether it is highly unlikely. They are ambivalent.

Your job is to get them to think that it is unlikely. In order to do this, you must understand what Professor Sandman calls "the seesaw." People will occupy the opposing side of your argument. You must try to occupy the major disaster seat. In order to do so, explain that, according to your assessment, if this happens, and this happens, and this happens, then a major environmental spill will occur. Then you show that the impacts would be dreadful. You focus on the terrible impacts until someone raises his or her hand to say: "But it is unlikely, right?" You can acknowledge but carry on with your sales pitch to get them to understand that your focus is on the terrible impacts. Your audience will eventually get fed up with you and start asking themselves why you are wasting their time with this unlikely scenario.

They will occupy the empty seat on the seesaw. They will focus on the unlikeliness of a major spill destroying pristine waters. Then, as a spokesperson for the government, you have them believing your truth: you want them to focus on the one-in-one-million scenario, the unlikely possibility of a spill. Professor Sandman has himself proclaimed that his approach to risk communication is profoundly counterintuitive and uncomfortable, both at the individual and organizational levels. It has challenged his clients' egos and their organizational cultures. They had powerful incentives to think his approach was reckless and to conclude that they need not do the things he was urging them to do. However, Professor Sandman was a successful consultant because he found ways to get through or past their resistance.

Whatever you do, do not try to convince your audience that it is ridiculous to think the worst-case scenario - a major disaster - can happen. The worst-case scenario is the position you want to occupy on the seesaw. If you go into the discussion armed with data to show that it is unlikely a major disaster will happen and you want to show that it is stupid to think it may happen, you are on the wrong track. Do not ever tell ambivalent people what you want them to believe.

Interestingly, the seesaw concept also works well when you want to defuse blame. Just think about how much more lenient you are when your child comes to you and tells you he broke the television remote, as opposed to you having to find the guilty party, with all your kids denying that they had anything to do with it. Taking the blame and apologizing usually reduces the degree of anger for the person who is the victim.

WHO CARES?

If as a spokesperson you really want to make the public angry, show them that you do not care. Lawrence G. Rawl, the petroleum engineer who was chairman and CEO of Exxon after the Exxon Valdez spill, did not show empathy. William K. Reilly, then head of the U.S. Environmental Protection Agency, said that Rawl *"provided a casebook example of how not to communicate to the public when your company messes up."*

During my tenure as an instructor at the Canadian Coast Guard College and as an International Maritime Organization instructor, I started to become interested in understanding stakeholders and the public as an audience. I needed to guide the on-scene commanders - those managing the disaster - when they had to talk to the media or rooms filled with angry stakeholders looking for blood. I would use the *Exxon Valdez* disaster to illustrate what to do and not to do, and what not to say when in front of a camera. You need to show you actually care. Be authentic, rather than focusing on showing that you will be someone who is great at engineering the cleanup.

The public expects Exxon to clean up. What the public wants to know is that Exxon feels guilty! The seesaw principle applies here as well. For example, if you, as the CEO, put the blame on yourself for the disaster, people will have a tendency to situate themselves on the other side of the seesaw and say: "Wait a minute here. The CEO can't be responsible for steering the ship onto the rocks." In contrast, if the CEO puts the blame on the master of the vessel, the public will occupy the other side of the seesaw: "How dare the CEO blame the master. He is the CEO. It is his company." A key phrase to use is: "My lawyers tell me we are not responsible, but I certainly feel responsible."

I had somewhat of a revelation as I took the Myers and Briggs psychology test. I began to understand why I was comfortable selling my truth and why other people, such as Lawrence Rawl of Exxon, were more comfortable being analytical and less emotional. Katherine Cook Briggs and her daughter, Isabel Briggs Myers, constructed the Myers-Briggs Type Indicator (MBTI). It is a self-reflective questionnaire. The results of the questionnaire indicate differing psychological preferences in how you perceive the world around you and how you make decisions. Since we all have a particular way of construing our experiences, the test demonstrates your preferences in terms of interests, needs, values, and motivational incentives. These four scales have some correlation with four of the Big Five personality traits, a framework you have probably encountered if your office is strong on helping team members define their personality and psyche. The framework is often represented by the acronyms OCEAN or CANOE, which stands for openness to experience, conscientious, extraversion, agreeableness, and neuroticism (ability to experience emotions like anger, anxiety, or depression).

The Myers and Briggs psychology test is one of many tests out there; most of the ones I have taken or taught are based on Carl Jung's work. Jung speculated that humans experience the world using four principal psychological functions: sensation, intuition, feeling, and thinking. Jung theorized that each person falls into one of two categories, the introvert and the extrovert. The introvert is thoughtful and insightful, focused on their internal world. While being reflective and vision-oriented, they can appear uninterested in joining your activities. The extrovert is the opposite, more focused on the outside world. The extrovert appears to be energetic. Introverts may find extroverts a bit too lively for their tastes or intimidating to their more introspective nature. (Jung, 1971)

You can characterize a person using different fundamental psychological attitudes, psychological constructs, or mental and emotional patterns. Attitudes are complex; we acquire them through experiences. An attitude is an individual's predisposed state of mind; it influences one's thoughts and actions. We form our attitudes from our past and present. We need to study attitudes in order to understand behaviour relationships. Jung's theory has become enormously influential in management theory when it comes to understanding workers' behaviours.

As a professional mariner, I had to be cognizant of my employees' attitudes and behaviours, as they inform how they react as workers. This was true not only to be a better manager, but also to be a good supervisor to prevent accidents. As chief officer, you are the supervisor of the watchkeepers, those assigned to navigate and pilot the ship. The master has the overall responsibility for piloting and navigating; the chief officer is, however, the supervisor of the deck staff, including the three navigation watch officers. On one particular voyage, the master and I had discussed how we needed to supervise the second officer who piloted between 1200-1600h and 0000-0400h. Our discussion was about the absentmindedness of the second officer who often lived in his own world. He was an outstanding person and knew the theoretical means to navigate and pilot better than most, but he was very much an introvert.

So many things could easily distract him that we had to double up his watch in areas that were easier to pilot. Difficult and challenging areas were not a problem, as he was stimulated and alert. But we worried in areas that were monotonous. Both the master and I would take turns checking in on him, each of us catching him nearly failing a few times during our month at sea.

It was a recent revelation for me that one's personality may be a cause or contributing factor to an accident. It was also a recent revelation that we might want to examine personalities when we interview parties to an accident. Further, I am a better communicator if I understand my audience, and I was a better investigator when I tried to understand the workers I was trying to convince to change their behaviour.

You will face a final challenge to communicate your knowledge. The public, your audience, will probably not read your report or listen or see you on the radio or television. They have retreated to information bubbles. People find their truth in *"self-curated information bubbles, where they read only that with which they agree, as if selecting their playlist for music."* (Edelman, 2018) If you are a spokesperson, you need to find out what your audience is reading and where they get their information.

WHOM TO TRUST?

The sociologist Georg Simmel claimed that trust is *"one of the most important synthetic forces within society"* (Möllering, 2001). Brad L. Rawlins, a researcher at the Institute for Public Relations, says, in similar words, that we need to trust if we are going to function in society. We also need to be trusted if we are going to be credible and have fulfilling experiences and relationships. Those in public relations jobs know that their success in communicating their truth is closely connected to the degree of trust their audience has in them. Communicators are in the trust-making business.

Research conducted by Markus Freitag and Richard Traunmüller (2009) from the University of Konstag in Germany has concluded that there are two types of trust. The first type is the intimate trust in people close to us. They call this particularized trust. The second type is an abstract trust in people in general, including strangers. They call this generalized trust. There is a logic to trust formation, whereby our trust encompasses a radius of experiences and predispositions. To build trust, we need to have positive experiences with strangers. We also need to have positive experiences with political institutions if we are to move from particularized trust to generalized trust. I would add that this is also true if you want to communicate your knowledge and you are a stranger to your audience and/or a government spokesperson.

Daniel J. McAllister, an associate professor in the Department of Management and Organization at the National University of Singapore, claims (1995) that there is a cognitive and affective approach to trust, with both being compatible dimensions rather than competitive ones. Cognitive-based trust depends on rational thought that is based on facts, whereas affect-based trust is based on an emotional connection, our degree of trust in a person given our relationship to that person. He found that levels of cognitive-based trust were higher than levels of affect-based trust and that some level of cognitive-based trust was necessary for affect-based trust to develop. Okay, however, I also think along a similar line as that espoused by Arthur Page, a former corporate public relations expert (Rawlings, 2007), who stated that building a relationship is *"90 percent doing and 10 percent talking."* I would therefore say that the affective approach to trust is more important than the cognitive approach. If you want to sell your truth, you need to build your trust with soft skills rather than focus on a strong scientific and technical message.

Psychological studies have shown that some people are taken more seriously than others, not because of their ability to sell themselves, but only because of their physical attributes. For example, tall people are more likely to have a successful career. Physical height is likely significantly related to self-esteem. It therefore makes sense to believe that someone tall would be perceived as having strong self-esteem and as inspiring confidence. We are more likely to trust people who are similar to us. Other studies have shown that there is a relationship between credibility and occupation. We place our trust in people in professions that appear to us to be credible, like doctors and scientists. To be trusted, an individual needs to be perceived as competent, reliable, and open; an individual needs to be perceived as caring about the needs of his or her audience.

The population's trust in politicians and belief that technocratic politics should be infallible has crumbled in the past decade, mainly because of events such as the Iraq war and the financial crisis. Remember Secretary of State Colin Powell showing us the deceptive news on Saddam Hussein hiding chemical weapons? For me, this is a landmark in the creation of public cynicism. Since then, doubt exists when government spokespeople try to sell us their knowledge.

Powell was considered a most credible spokesperson around the world. He now claims that the CIA deceived him, but it is too late. If Powell can deceive, what does it mean for the other spokespeople? The public was always skeptical, but skepticism is growing even greater nowadays. A form of collapse in the establishment is occurring. People give more and more credence to radical movements such as that of the anti-vaxxers. Some public spokespeople are demonized. Political leaders are doubted, and this doubt spills over into scientific disciplines where empirical evidence is necessary to sell the truth. Investigators are not spared. The public's trust in experts and elites is plunging.

Following the Fukushima Daiichi nuclear accident (2011), Dr. Vincent Covello, from the Center for Change and Risk Communication in the U.S., provided a credibility ladder in a presentation that he made to the international experts' meeting on radiation protection. The credibility ladder compares the degree of credibility of different individuals involved in disasters. At the top of the credibility scale are citizen or stakeholder panels, nurses, physicians, and other health professionals. At the bottom of the scale, conspicuously present, as expected, are industry officials and consultants from for-profit firms. Is this still the case today? What about accident investigators, do we trust them?

Each year, since 2001, Edelman Intelligence, a global insight and analytics consultancy, has produced the Edelman Trust Barometer. The 2018 edition of the barometer shows a dramatic drop in trust in the U.S. In fact, the U.S. suffered the largest-ever drop in trust in their survey history among the general public. There is a correlation between this drop and a lack of faith in government. Workplace accident investigators need to be cognizant of what this drop in trust means to them, given that most investigators are public servants.

The drop recorded by the 2018 barometer is the first time that there has been a drop in trust without a simultaneous catastrophic event, like the Fukushima nuclear disaster, or a pressing economic issue. The media is the least trusted institution globally. The majority of us (59 percent) claim that we are unable to identify the truth in media stories. The most trusted spokespeople come from the technical field (63 percent) followed by academics (61 percent). The public is trusted at only 54 percent. Unsurprising to me, and probably to you too, is that our trust in spokespeople varies from country to country. Further, for Americans, trust in spokespeople varies depending on where the company is headquartered. A company headquartered in Canada gets a trust rating of 68 percent, whereas a company headquartered in Mexico or India gets a trust rating of 32 percent. Troublingly, close to 7 in 10 respondents to the Edelman survey worry that fake news and false information can be used as a weapon. We are in a new era and a scary one indeed. This means spokespeople trying to sell their truth to the public need to understand the landscape even better.

So, new to us in 2018 is the situation where we no longer think that our peers - people who resemble us - are the most believable source of information. The bright side is that this is good news for investigators of all types; there is a renewed confidence in experts and academics. But wait: the data collected refers to technical experts but does not talk about investigators. I made an intellectual leap that is probably inaccurate. Data can be difficult to interpret, as Mark Twain once pointed out in one of his famous quotes: *"Lies, damned lies, and statistics."* Investigators may be experts, but at times they are spokespeople as well, or someone else speaks on their behalf. Also, investigators are not technical experts when it comes to providing knowledge about human conflict and social interactions, or comment on how work-is-done versus how work-was-imagined. Investigators may be communicating a point of view.

Nevertheless, it is safe to assume that the average person links investigators with the government, which has been affected by a significant drop in trust - 30 percent, according to Edelman. Fewer than one in three citizens believe that government officials are credible. These are staggering numbers. This means that more than 2 out of 3 people who read this book will not think I am credible given my past as a government official. Thank you to the less than one of three.

The landscape in which investigators operate changed again in 2019. The entire landscape is in flux, but it remains clear that public officials are taking a hit. The 2019 Edelman Trust Barometer revealed that people have shifted their trust to the relationships within their control, most notably the relationships with their employers: *"Globally, 75% of people trust "my employer" to do what is right, significantly more than NGOs (57%), business (56%) and media (47%)."* (Edelman, 2019)

Trust in societal institutions has been in progressive decline for the past two decades as *"a consequence of the Great Recession, fears about immigration and economic dislocation caused by globalization and automation."* We have seen how CEOs and heads of state discredit themselves. The general population continues to distrust institutions (49 percent) and women are more skeptical than men. This low confidence has you and I turn to our employers, at a rate of 75% of respondents, a whopping 19 percent more than business in general and 27 percent more than government. (Edelman, 2019)

Nik Nanos, the chief data scientist at Nanos Research, reported the results to a question about how Canadians feel about their federal government in Ottawa. The numbers were bleak. He found that 23 percent responded they are angry; 27 percent responded they are pessimistic; and, 8 percent responded they are disinterested. Only 18 percent say they are optimistic and 16 percent say they are satisfied. (Nanos, 2018) With these numbers in mind, imagine representing the government when you need to sell knowledge about an accident.

CLOSING ARGUMENTS

We have seen that people (including representatives) lie and deceive which may taint the way they perceive spokespeople. The public could think you are voluntarily or involuntarily deceiving them. You have also seen that your audience may see you as someone trying to sell them knowledge that does not fit their reality. You need to know your audience and determine how best to tailor and deliver your message. You need to both develop knowledge about the accident - which we have shown you how to do in Chapters

I to III - and determine how you communicate the reality you have created.

You need to know where people stand on issues and what they care about. You need to find out what information they filter out and in what echo chamber they situate themselves. You need to know what reality they find themselves in, and in what created reality they live.

Creating reality has been studied extensively. The first to undertake the study was David Hume, a Scottish philosopher who wrote on the nature of imaginative creation in the 18th century. Hume examined the psychological basis of human nature and claimed that passion, rather than reason, governs human behaviour. For Hume, our trust in causality and induction is the result of customs and mental habits. When we look at the way we create reality today, we find that reality is what our social network thinks. We determine the truth based on our network, a social construct, which is increasingly linked to social media. Citizens today are just a mouse click away from mobilizing, mostly against realities external to their network.

If you want to communicate knowledge, share your truth, you must remember that people want to know you care before you can even try to tell them what you care about - emotions before facts. And not only do people want to know you care, but even more importantly, they want you to listen to them. Presenting your truth should not be about you, your knowledge, and your message. It has to be about your audience, how they feel, and what they care about. Tony Hayward of BP learned the hard way during the crisis of the oil rig *Deepwater Horizon*. You, on the other hand, now know that you can take the time to reflect on the emotions you want to convey before disaster strikes or sitting at a press conference releasing your report.

To increase the chance that your findings will be acted upon, you must show your audience that you are caring, a great listener, and capable of empathy and compassion. You also need to show that you understand what your audience cares about. You must get this message across very rapidly before you even think about introducing the knowledge you want to convey. Honesty and expertise are important, but they come second, after empathy. Selling a dry and technical narrative will most likely be ineffective unless you appeal to the emotional side of your audience.

Conclusion

The End Game Is Improving People's Lives
Working Toward a New Meaningful Investigation Model

We are in Seattle, WA, 2006. The vice-president of aircraft programs at Boeing is briefing the board of directors: *"We are considering replacing the most successful airline jet, our 737, with a new model, starting with a clean sheet design that would follow our 787 Dreamliner."* The idea is appealing, but Boeing postpones the decision to 2011.

In the meantime, a barrel of oil settles above $61 marking another tough year for energy consumers but a great year for the petroleum industry. It is the fifth straight year of oil price increases. Analysts are looking for crude futures to average more than $60 a barrel again the following year. There is robust growth in demand in Asia and the Middle East. OPEC tries to trim the supply, creating market-rattling instability in energy-rich countries such as Nigeria and Iraq. The price hike somewhat stabilizes and averages at about $62 in 2009.

However, in January 2010, the Energy Information Administration in New York predicts the West Texas crude prices will average about $80 over the year and about $84 in 2011. It appears that the world oil market will tighten as the global economic recovery continues after the 2007-08 financial crisis. The prediction comes through; the price of oil averages $71.21 in 2010 and $87.04 in '11.

Let's go back to 2006 for a moment, this time in Toulouse, France. The head of development at Airbus prepares to brief his board of directors. Over breakfast, he is thrilled to see that his Toulouse football team has a line-up that may finally reap a winning season. He muses about the fact that he predicts the team will do well in 2007. He puts down the paper and looks at his briefing notes. He also sees the next generation of planes as being memorable. He smiles and prepares his briefing, planning to use a football analogy as a sales pitch.

He kicks off his presentation: *"We are launching today the A320 Enhanced (A320E) program, a series of modifications that will improve fuel efficiency. We are confident to improve fuel consumption by 4 to 5 percent. We are optimistic that we could add another 10 percent in the next decade with new engine technology. I am absolutely certain that Airbus, like our football club, is on track to make history."*

On December 1, 2010, Airbus launches the A320neo (New Engine Option), scheduling it to enter into service less than six years later. It will feature a new PW1000G engine, built by Pratt and Whitney, and provide 16 percent less fuel consumption. The head of development was right during his 2006 briefing, both about the plane and the Toulouse football club (finishes third and earns a place in the 2007-08 UEFA Champions League third qualifying round). The A320neo family would generate more than 6,500 orders by the beginning of 2019, making them a huge success.

In early January 2011, amidst the oil price crisis, the Indian low-cost carrier Indigo orders 180 of the A320 series. Shortly after, on January 17, we read that Virgin America has ordered 90 of the same series of A320s to become what they claim to be the first commercial order for the new eco-efficient engine option. The company goes on to state: *"Virgin America is the launch customer for the new eco-efficient Airbus A320neo aircraft, which promises to be one of the most fuel and carbon-efficient commercial aircraft in the world"* (Virgin America, 2011). The race is on between Airbus and Boeing to capture the most lucrative part of the market share in the category of airplanes that carry between 140 and 180 passengers. The race actually started earlier, but this public announcement by Virgin America is a key milestone.

On July 20 in Paris, American Airlines announces it *"plans to acquire 460 narrowbody, single-aisle aircraft from the 737 and Airbus A320 families beginning in 2013 through 2022 - the largest aircraft order in aviation history."* This order breaks the longstanding monopoly that Boeing had with American Airlines and signals that Boeing is entering the race with Airbus. Boeing plans to revamp its 737 with new engines that go against the preferred option of its customers in order to create a completely new aircraft.

Saj Ahmad, an analyst at FBE Aerospace in London, was quoted in the *New York Times* as having said, *"Not only have they [Airbus] sold jets to American, but they have forced Boeing's hand into pushing for a re-engined 737."* Howard Wheeldon, senior strategist at BGC Partners, a London brokerage, was also quoted in the *Times*: *"This is significant for Airbus, but even more significant for Boeing."* Boeing, he said, had been "chastened" by the market response to the A320neo, *"which is making better headway than anyone had expected."* Mr. Ahmad was quoted as agreeing: *"Boeing has said for months it wouldn't rush to a decision. But now that they have had to react to this deal, they, too, will capture new swathes of orders"* (Clark, 2011).

The decisions by these airlines to move to new aircraft could mean the reduction in overall fuel bills by 15 percent at the time of AMR's decision (AMR Corporation owned American Airlines in 2011). The effect of fuel cost on the bottom line is clear. For companies that paid an average of $3.12 a gallon for jet fuel, this is up 32 percent from an average of $2.37 a gallon in the period a year earlier. AMR alone could be impacted up to $524 million, offsetting gains in revenue.

In the weekly newsmagazine *Flight International* of September 11, 2011, Niall O'Keeffe writes about Boeing having two options. The first is to go with a new build and *"take on the enormous expense and engineering burden that an all-new type would entail."* The second is to take a *"pragmatic attitude"* and modify the 737 to keep *"pace with its rival in performance, timeframe and cost terms"* (O'Keeffe, 2011). Boeing abandons the development of a new design. The board approves the announcement on August 30 to launch the re-engined 737 with a catalogue order of 496 airplanes from five airlines.

The 737 MAX should burn less fuel than its competitor aircraft and meet or exceed its range. The heavier engines will be located further forward and higher than the previous ones. This means the introduction of a new Maneuvering Characteristics Augmentation System (MCAS) to mitigate the pitch tendency of the new flight geometry. The new system prevents stalls in flaps-retracted, low-speed, nose-up flight. The MCAS uses sensor data to compute when a dangerous condition has emerged and then trims the aircraft nose down.

I have provided a somewhat cursory explanation of the events and business environment that led to the creation of the 737 MAX. These aircraft were certified, and we believed they were safe when they went into service. However, as it may be vivid in your memory, on October 29, 2018, the Lion Air Flight 610 plunged into the Java Sea shortly after take-off from the airport in Jakarta, Indonesia, killing all 189 passengers and crew. On March 10, 2019, Ethiopian Airline Flight 302 also crashed shortly after take-off from Addis Ababa, Ethiopia, killing all 157 passengers and crew.

What we know is the vertical speed for the Flight 302 aircraft after take-off was unstable. Investigators have retrieved evidence so far to suggest that both aircraft were configured to dive at the time of the crash. Why? My goal is not to belabour why these airplanes dived and crashed. I am not investigating and will not draw conclusions in an area where I do not hold any expertise, aircraft construction and operations. I present this case study to show you a sample of issues that compose the system that creates a new aircraft that crashed on two separate occasions. This can help us identify some potential areas to investigate.

What socio-economic scenarios played out from 2006 onwards that influenced the creation of the Boeing aircraft? Is there any political lobbying or influence within the USA that negatively affects the design and construction of aircraft competing with European designs? What parts of the business environment might have deleteriously influenced the decision to modify an aircraft in lieu of starting from scratch? We probably will never get answers to these questions. Investigation bodies rarely venture, if ever, to understand the elements that generate industrial builds, work environments, and processes leading to accidents and incidents.

This is one reason why I decided to write this essay. My experience and education allowed me to believe that we were not going far enough in some of our investigations. We were excellent in identifying the immediate causes and contributing factors that lead to disasters, but we were not very proficient in studying the systems that create disasters. I wanted to research what we were doing right and identify areas where we were failing.

EXAMINING THE EVIDENCE

Accident investigators will know why the 737 MAX planes crashed based on the science and techniques I explained in the first three chapters. I have demonstrated throughout the book the need to dig deeper to understand the system that gives way to these occurrences. This part, digging deeper, includes looking at performance, non-events, and how work-is-done. I am introducing you to areas that are typically not investigated thoroughly.

We can stop more 737 MAXes from inducing a dive, but we may not be able to describe the system that created the aircraft. To prevent more disasters from happening, we may need to identify underlying causes and contributing factors that lead to the in-service operation of new aircraft. We should try to understand the systems that create machines, plants, and high-tech engineering projects.

I began this book by showing you how we all make errors, how we all fail. I then explained how accidents happen and how investigators conduct their work. I demonstrated that we accumulate knowledge when we investigate, but not necessarily the truth that can improve safety. Finally, I teased you with some notions on communicating the truth. We saw that we can determine what causes accidents, but we may not be telling the story needed to prevent further disasters from happening.

If the end game is improving people's lives (e.g., having more robust transportation systems), we need to do a better job of understanding how society is woven together. We need to understand that our social workings are not just about *logos*, but also *pathos*, probably even more about pathos. We are, after all, beings that find more comfort in associating with each other for the emotional connection we gain than for the knowledge we exchange.

Science will never allow us to achieve absolute truth; it cannot translate the objective world into absolute truth. Can we therefore say there is a truth? I hope that, after reading this book, you are drawing the conclusion that there can be many truths, or at least never just one truth.

What's true? What's false? In case you haven't noticed, the world has pretty much given up on the old Enlightenment idea of piecing together the truth based on observed data. Reality is too complicated and scary for that. Instead, it's way easier to ignore all data that doesn't fit your preconceptions and believe all data that does. I believe what I believe, and you believe what you believe, and we'll agree to disagree. It's liberal tolerance meets Dark Ages denialism (Hill, 2017).

Researchers and investigators need to be wise and, as much as possible, objective - detaching themselves from the object of interest in order to draw a conclusion with the utmost impartiality. Before searching for truth, one must have the desire to find the truth. Investigators must also understand the environment in which they are communicating their findings. They are not very good at doing this. They do not usually, if ever, consider the social, economic, and political environment in which the accident occurred and in which they are trying to communicate their findings.

Western decision-making is under stress because policy wonks (decision-makers) have not understood - or conceived - that the system is a system. They make decisions without understanding the environment in which they want to apply their policies. Is it even possible to develop a workable model of an industrial environment or a social environment when we know that we are working with open systems - systems that do not have finite limits? How do we conceive of a model considering that social values continuously evolve and affect our workplaces, and workplaces themselves continuously evolve?

Creating a new workable investigation model may be the next challenge for investigators in the field of industrial accidents and those in similar investigation fields, such as coroners. The past few decades have been spent sifting through the surface, digging at the top socio-economic layers that were uncovered because of the theoretical models presented in Chapter II. We have picked the low-hanging fruit: wear your safety equipment, develop training programs, and implement a safety culture in the workplace.

We ask primary questions to determine, for example, if the company or government should have safety management systems. The answer has been the obvious yes. Accident investigation bodies have been harping on this finding and other macroscopic findings for a long time now, mainly since the Chernobyl and *Herald of Free Enterprise* (passenger vessel capsize) disasters in the late 1980s. Nevertheless, we still have accidents where we find the same easily solvable causes and contributing factors. Why?

For one, rudimentary errors continue to occur (e.g., slips, lapses, and mistakes) and some unscrupulous company owners are not living up to expectation and are failing in their obligation to ensure a safe environment for their workers. Perhaps we are not making as much headway anymore because of the way we are set up to investigate. There is still a need to investigate using traditional causal and epidemiological models to uncover the most obvious causes, contributing factors, and risks. We need to find the immediate causes of the 737 MAX airplane disasters. But I venture that the time has come to dig deeper in order to better understand the socio-economic environment in which accidents happen. It is now essential to understand the system that surrounds the production of work environments and new builds. We need to better understand the system that creates disasters.

We need to do two things. First, we need to acknowledge that investigation bodies around the world are not set up to study the systems. Second, we need to develop a workable model that allows researchers and practitioners to dig deep down to uncover the next level of underlying factors that will permit us to understand how the evolving systems are affected and work.

Investigators are excellent at uncovering knowledge using traditional models even though they may sometimes construct debatable findings. Investigators' conclusions can become shaky as soon as they toe the line of interpreting anything related to neo-Marxist conflict or underlying economic or political causes and contributing factors. When an investigation needs to delve into human factors, an area that is extremely complex, it most likely will need to recruit the help of specialized researchers in various human sciences.

Investigation bodies need to understand the limits of their staff and need to draw a line between simple linear and complex linear investigations with systemic investigations. The latter need multi-disciplinary experts, large amounts of money, and acknowledgment that it will take a lot more time to produce a final report.

We need to acknowledge that we have not yet found a comprehensive workable model for investigating in our post-modern world. There are many reasons for this. First, investigators are not always aware of the limits of their work and therefore they are not raising an alarm about their confusion. Second, there is no dialogue between investigators and researchers. Third, investigation bodies are structured according to national legislation that is often based on international conventions elaborated by policy wonks predominantly using the epidemiological linear model. We are at least a generation away from agreeing internationally that we need to restructure investigation bodies. We need to re-examine the way we accumulate knowledge.

We require professionals investigating professionals (e.g., airline pilots investigating airline pilots) and human factors specialists examining the social, political and economic workings of the system. The latter group needs to be given free rein to produce independent findings that encompass social, economic, and political factors.

THE "WHODUNIT" EFFECT

Reorganization of investigation bodies may not occur until we can agree that a new model to explain accidents is needed, one that shows that small changes have larger effects, a bit like the butterfly effect. The butterfly effect postulates the sensitive dependence on initial conditions; when there is a small change in one state of a deterministic nonlinear system, large differences in a later state can result.

Edward Lorenz coined the term *butterfly effect* from the example of the details of the exact time of formation and path taken by a tornado, influenced by minor perturbations such as the flapping of the wings of a distant butterfly way before the creation of the weather event. Lorenz discovered his chaos theory after observing that patterns of his weather model seeded with initial condition data that rounded in an inconsequential manner would fail to reproduce the results of runs with the unrounded initial condition data. A minute change in initial conditions would create a significantly different outcome.

Lorenz gave a name to the phenomenon. However, French mathematician and engineer Henri Poincaré and American mathematician and philosopher Norbert Wiener first recognized the idea that small causes may have large effects in general and in weather specifically. Lorenz's work situated the concept of the instability of the earth's atmosphere on a quantitative base. He linked the concept of instability to the properties of large classes of dynamic systems, which are undergoing nonlinear dynamics and deterministic chaos. (Lorenz, 1963)

I am not saying that we should try to identify all the deterministic and minute changes that may affect a worker's environment, like the flapping of wings from a passing butterfly or the identification of a successful Toulouse football team line-up before Airbus announces a new aircraft. However, I am saying that nonlinear dynamics and deterministic chaos affect a worker's environment.

To change the system and improve safety, we need to uncover some of the microscopic and macroscopic nonlinear dynamics.

Yuval Noah Harari is a historian and lecturer at the Hebrew University of Jerusalem. In *Sapiens*, an international bestseller, he provides his own explanation of chaotic systems. He notes that they come in two levels. The first level is chaos that does not react to predictions about the studied phenomena. The best example of this type of chaos is the weather. So many factors influence the weather that even the computer models that consider a myriad of variables cannot help meteorologists provide consistent accurate predictions.

The second level of chaos reacts to predictions about the studied phenomena. That definition does not sound very chaotic, so let me explain by using the example of the market price of gold. If we were able to develop a computer program that forecasts the exact moment with 100 percent accuracy that one ounce of gold would be worth $2,000 tomorrow, the price would not materialize because the stock market would react to the prediction and affect its outcome. Traders would rush to purchase gold, and the price would in fact rise to $2,000 today. We could not know what would happen tomorrow.

Both chaotic levels exist in a worker's environment. Nonlinear dynamics and deterministic chaos affect a worker's environment or the decisions that lead to the creation of a new aircraft such as the 737 MAX. On March 19, 2019, the U.S. Department of Transportation requested the Office of the Inspector General conduct an audit on the 737 MAX certification process. On March 29, 2019, we learned from Thomas Kaplan of the New York Times that an internal watchdog had looked at the part of the Federal Aviation Administration (FAA) responsible for certifying the new Boeing jetliners in 2013 and came to some troubling conclusions: *"FAA employees viewed their management ... as having too close a relationship with Boeing officials."* Kaplan continued on to question if the *"FAA has gone too far in allowing Boeing to regulate itself"* (Kaplan, 2019).

The conditions surrounding the construction of a new airplane included a highly competitive environment, high fuel prices, and a certification process under scrutiny. These are all components of what I consider the first level of chaos. The Inspector General and investigative journalists may be able to provide us with a partial understanding of the socio-economic political system that led to the creation of the 737 MAX. However, I do not think we will ever get a true overall picture that would allow us to determine the root causes in order to apply our learning to mitigate the next transport or industry disaster.

I am doubtful that we will ever get a proper picture of the system that was in place that created the conditions to build and certify an aircraft that suddenly dives and crashes. We need to understand the *whodunit* effect, the microscopic and macroscopic nonlinear dynamics, the chaos that generates industrial builds, work environments, and processes leading to accidents and incidents.

CLOSING ARGUMENTS

The first thing I wanted to achieve in this essay is to demonstrate what can be summed up by a quote from Dr. Stephen Blank's Foreword: *"The danger is that our stories become too neat, leading inevitably to the conclusion, and missing the vital elements of uncertainty, doubt and confusion at the time. This is why the search for the culprit in an accident investigation can blind us to the wider factors that shaped the accident."* Pursuing this endeavour, I showed you that we cannot find a single-point failure; we cannot find someone to blame for an accident.

I have taken you on a journey to explain the difficulties in identifying causes and contributing factors after an accident because our work environments are highly complex, comprising various perspectives and cultural backgrounds that affect the way we organize, interact, and participate in our daily tasks. The challenges of investigating are compounded by the countless, often hidden, political and economic decisions that influence what we do and why we do things, such as whether or not to purchase safety equipment and whether or not to take risks, such as shortcuts, in order to cut exploitation costs.

I have also tried in this book to enlist you in my mindset, bring you to agree with me that it is time to review the way we investigate failure. We may have reached the end of an era, a time to rethink many areas of society. I claim that doing so, we should examine if accident investigators need theoretical models that explain the societal paradigm at the source of occupational accidents.

To identify the root causes of accidents, it may even be necessary to focus our research using the theoretical understanding covered in Chapter III. I mentioned that social movements (e.g., the feminist movement or ecological movement) could help improve the field of work-related accident investigation. It may be that we eventually discover that we have to reorient the economy and the social environment to reshape the culture of companies in order to reduce accidents at work.

Finally, this essay touched on the way "truth" is perceived by the stakeholders with whom investigators are trying to induce change. When investigators start on their task to acquire knowledge about a workplace accident, their goal is to stop similar accidents from happening. They are not searching for a culprit. They need to communicate their findings and initiate change, often a change in stakeholder behaviour. This task is colossal for two reasons.

The first is that we live in a world of lies and deceit. We all lie and deceive, sometimes involuntarily and unknowingly. This environment creates a twisted challenge where investigators need to sell their debatable knowledge to people that are already cynical and also lie and deceive themselves.

The second reason is that people are biased. They process information and form their beliefs about knowledge based on their prior attitudes. They select and evaluate knowledge more positively when it supports their existing beliefs and attitudes. People tend to consider new knowledge based on their perceptions, feelings, and values. Investigators need to understand the emotional status of their stakeholders.

Investigators become risk communicators when they publish their findings. Risk communicators commonly resort to two tactics: scaring people, because the public is complacent about a danger or, alternatively, reassuring people, because the public is upset about the magnitude and probability of an event when in actuality the danger level is low. Risk communicators manage concern, fear and anger, and play with the perception of risk. Acquiring and applying these skills is a challenge, especially when we know that investigators often communicate their knowledge to a skeptical crowd.

I end this book in the same manner I started it, sharing some thoughts on the concept of doubt and our quest for the truth. We tend to take our safety for granted and assume that accidents will not occur. We have all felt a sense of disbelief when an accident materializes: "I never thought it would happen to me." We must doubt our ability as humans to work without making errors. This could allow us to learn about a chaotic system that can be conducive to creating an incident or an accident. We should also doubt our ability to accurately translate a social construct made up of known objective phenomena and a network of subjective consciousness and beliefs.

There is never a universal truth and there never will be. Winning the truth battle is not what is important. You have to determine what you are trying to achieve. If your goal is to improve safety in the workplace, you may have to put aside your evidence-based work. Focus on the audience's perceptions, feelings, and values. This may be the only way you succeed in initiating change in people's habits and customs.

Before you craft and communicate your findings, start by accepting that the knowledge you have is not the absolute truth. You may think you know *"whodunit,"* but so does the audience. Both may have it right in a world that has become unintelligible.

Appendix
Notes and References

FOREWORD

Dahir, Abdi Latif. "Captain in Mauritius Oil Spill Disaster Is Arrested". *The New York Times*. August 18, 2020.

Carr, Edward Hallett. What Is History? London: Macmillan, 1961; revised edition ed. R.W. Davies, Harmondsworth: Penguin, 1986.

PREFACE

I mention Jacob Bronowski, a British mathematician and historian of science, who wrote and presented the 1973 British Broadcasting Corporation, Time-Life Productions series (13 episodes) called *The Ascent of Man*.

CHAPTER I

The account of the *Concordia* accident on CTV news (Canadian Press, Friday, April 2, 2010): https://www.ctvnews.ca/microburst-hit-sailing-school-tall-ship-expert-1.498357 (Last accessed August 1, 2020). This is also where I extracted the quotes. The investigation report about the sail training vessel *Concordia* can be found at www.tsb.gc.ca: M10F0003.

A video of the Uber car accident is available on several websites, including CNBC, https://www.cnbc.com/2018/03/21/uber-pedestrian-accident-tempe-police-release-video.html (Last accessed August 1, 2020).

I chose to cover errors using the classification scheme associated with slips and mistakes. There are other ways to classify errors; some use a system that divides errors into random, systematic, and sporadic, for example. I selected the system that I found easiest to use in order to explain the types of errors that we all normally commit each day and that provides sufficient examples to show how clumsy we can be.

The theory reproduced in this chapter was extracted from the following books that form the best section in accident investigators' libraries.

- Edwards, E. Man and Machine: Systems for safety. Proceedings of the BALPA Technical Symposium, London. 1972.

- Hawkins, F.H. Human Factors in Flight. Aldershot, UK: Gower Technical Press. 1987.

- Nagel, D.C. Human Error in Aviation Operations. In E.L. Weiner and D.C. Nagel (Eds.), Human Factors in Aviation (pp. 263-303). San Diego, CA: Academic Press. 1988.

- Norman, D.A. Categorization of Action Slips, Psychological Review, 88 (1), 1-15. 1981.

- Norman, D.A. The Psychology of Everyday Things. New York: Basic Books. 1988.

- Rasmussen, J. The definition of human error and a taxonomy for technical system design. In J. Rasmussen, K. Duncan, and J. Leplat (Eds.), New Technology and Human Error. Toronto: John Wiley & Sons. 1987.

- Reason, J. Human Error. New York: Cambridge University Press. 1990.

The following references helped me pepper the section with other thoughts and theories.

- "Gestalt," definition, Random House Webster's Unabridged Dictionary.

- Koffka, K. Principles of Gestalt Psychology. 1935. p. 176.

· Giuffrida, Angela. "Genoa bridge death toll rises to 35 as more bodies are pulled from rubble". *The Guardian*. August 15, 2018. Retrieved April 4, 2019.

· Heider, F. (1977). Cited in Dewey, R.A. Psychology: An introduction, Chapter 4, The Whole Is Other Than the Sum of the Parts. 2007.

· Shappell, S.; Wiegmann, D. The human factors analysis and classification system - HFACS, DOT/FAA/AM-00/7, Office of Aviation Medicine, Federal Aviation Administration, Department of Transport. 2000.

· Wiegmann, D.; Shappell, S. A human error approach to aviation accident analysis: The human factors analysis and classification system. Ashgate. 2003.

CHAPTER II

You may want to read the following authors in sequence of publication date for more on what constitutes an error.

Senders and Moray (1991, p. 25) mention that an error is *"something that has been done which was not intended by the actor, not desired by a set of rules or an external observer, or that led the task or system outside its acceptable limits."*

Woods, Johannesen, Cook, and Sarter (1994, p. 2) also have definitions of errors that, to me, are less appealing. For them, an error is *"a specific variety of human performance that is so clearly and significantly substandard and flawed when viewed in retrospect that there is no doubt that it should have been viewed by the practitioner as substandard at the time the act was committed or omitted."* I do not find this definition as interesting because the cause of an accident may include many cumulative errors that are not so clearly and significantly substandard or flawed.

Finally, a third reference can be found at http://wikiofscience. wikidot.com/quasiscience:error. Strauch (2004, p. 21) says that error can be defined as *"an action or decision that results in one or more unintended negative outcomes"*. I fully agree with this definition.

· Perrow, C. "The President's Commission and the Normal Accident," in Sills, D.; Wolf, C.; and Shelanski, V. (Eds), Accident at Three Mile Island: The Human Dimensions, Westview, Boulder, pp. 173-184. 1982.

· Senders, J.W. and Moray, N.P. Human Error: Cause, Prediction, and Reduction. Lawrence Erlbaum Associates. Hillsdale, NJ. 172 pages. 1991.

· Strauch, B. Investigating Human Error: Incidents, Accidents, and Complex Systems. Ashgate Pub. Ltd. 2004.

· Woods, D.D.; Johannesen, L.; Cook, R.I.; and Sarter, N.B. Behind Human Error: Cognitive Systems, Computers and Hindsight. Crew Systems Ergonomic Information and Analysis Center, WPAFB, Dayton OH. 1994.

The investigation report about the *MSC Monica* can be found at www.tsb.gc.ca: M16C0005.

There are many models and methods used to identify risks and establish defences. There are also many tools to help measure performance. Specialists may be interested in the Functional Resonance Analysis Method (FRAM) or the Resilience Analysis Matrix (RAM), both of which can be used to visualize functional dependencies in complex socio-technical systems. The methods help understand the planned work versus the work actually done, and model system behaviour. You can find many in-depth analysis methods and tree-based techniques, including Fault Tree Analysis, Event Tree Analysis, and the Management Oversight Risk Tree (MORT). You can easily enrich your acronym collection when you tally all the available tools: FMEA (Failure Mode and Effect Analysis); FMECA (Failure Mode Effect and Criticality Analysis); HACCP (Hazard Analysis Control Critical Point); HAZOP (Hazard and Operability Study); and PRA (Preliminary Risk Analysis).

For more on tools, see Amalberti, René (2013), a professor of medicine, physiology, and ergonomics, who is known for his research in the medical field on medical errors, patient safety, system approach, and resilience.

· Amalberti, R. Navigating Safety: Necessary Compromises and Trade-Offs - Theory and Practice. Springer Science and Business Media. 2013.

I cover some ground on social relations not usually studied by investigators. We intuitively know a lot from our day-to-day encounters or from searching for explanations for various deportments and group dynamics. During my undergraduate studies, I minored in sociology. The program covered two semesters and helped me to be more introspective. I gleaned more than a few kernels of wisdom from the teachings of Max Weber, Émile Durkheim, and Alfred Schutz.

Weber is a German sociologist and one of the founders of the science of sociology, along with Karl Marx and Durkheim. I regularly go back to Weber's teachings. From Weber, I learned the foundation of sociology and a definition of sociology that I used in my work as an investigator. It goes something like this: Sociology is the attempt to interpret our understanding of social action to arrive at a causal explanation of its course and effects. We must consider all actions taken by humans as behaviours when the actor attaches a subjective meaning to them. Our actions are social insofar as they have consequences on the behaviour of others.

From Durkheim, a French sociologist, I learned that it is possible to explain a worker's environment and derive sociological explanations by doing statistical correlations. Durkheim introduced the theory of social integration, which looks at the means by which people connect, interact, and confirm each other within a community. Describing social integration is a way of describing the established patterns in societal relations.

Schutz is an Austrian-born U.S. sociologist and philosopher who developed a social science based on phenomenology, a 19th-century movement whose primary objective was to direct investigations and descriptions of phenomena as we consciously experience them. According to Schutz, we create, in our everyday actions, a social reality through symbols and human action. We should investigate and describe what we see as freely as possible from examined preconceptions and presumptions. Schutz laid the basis for the study of our common-sense understandings of the structure of social interaction.

Resilience engineering, an interesting concept not covered in this chapter, is used by practitioners of phenomenology when they try to understand the framework of risk in order to develop security procedures in complex systems. They replace workers' actions as units of measurement by the practices of the workers. The result is that they consider the worker and his or her environment as one unit structured according to the results they need to achieve. There are similar theories that use a mixture of Marxist philosophy and American pragmatism.

Resilience engineering is an innovative paradigm shift useful in many areas, including in complex health care systems. The goal with resilience engineering is to describe various ways - methods - to safely produce a product or a procedure.

You may want to get to know Tom Dwyer's Weberian interpretation. To be valid, an explanation must be appropriate both causally and meaningfully. Causal relationships can be established using observations, statistics, and data. In meaningful relationships workers undertake actions in an informed way for a particular purpose. For an explanation to be validated, the workers themselves must accept it. In other words, findings must be reviewed and accepted by the people affected if they are going to reap any benefit.

In this chapter, I use the word "struggle" in the neo-Marxist sense. For example, struggle can refer to a conflict between the culture of the workers and what governments and employers expect of them.

· Audet, M., Landry, M., Déry, R., Sciences et résolution de problème : liens, difficultés et voies de dépassement dans les champs des sciences de l'administration, Philosophie des sciences sociales, 1986, vol. 16, p. 409-440.

· Audet, M., Larouche, V., Paradigmes, écoles de pensée et théories en relations industrielles, Relations Industrielles, 1988, vol. 43, no 1, p. 3-31.

· Bélanger, P.R. et Lévesque, B. 1994 "Modernisation sociale des entreprises : diversité des configurations et modèle québécois," P.R. Bélanger, M. Grant, B. Lévesque, La modernisation sociale des entreprises, Montréal, Presses de l'Université de Montréal, p. 17-52.

· Blain, A.N., Gennard, J., "Industrial Relations Theory: A Critical Review," British Journal of Industrial Relations, 1970, No. 3.

· Boivin, Jean. Introduction aux relations industrielles. 2e édition. Gaëtan Morin Éditeur. 2010.

· Bridges, Karl, E.; Corballis, Paul, M.; Hollnagel, Erik. "Failure-to-Identify" hunting incidents: a resilience engineering approach. Sage Journals. January 23, 2018.

· Conklin, T. Pre-Accident Investigations: An introduction to organizational safety, CRC Press: Taylor & Francis Group. 2012.

· Déry, R., La structuration de l'épistémologie contemporaine, Montréal, HEC, Cahier de recherche no 91-04, 47 p.

· Dunlop, J.T., Industrial Relations Systems, New York, Henry Holt, 1958.

· Dodier, N., Life and Death at Work: Industrial accidents as a case of socially produced error, a review of the book by T. Dwyer in Sociologie française de sociologie, Vol. 33, No. 4 (Oct- Dec. 1992), pp. 670-673.

· Dwyer, T., The Production of Industrial Accidents: A sociological approach, The Journal of Sociology, New Zealand, 1981. Vol. 17. No. 2, pp. 59-65.

· Dwyer, T., Life and Death at Work: Industrial accidents as a case of socially produced error, Plenum Press, New York and London, 1991.

· Dekker, S. Malicious compliance. In HindSight 25. No. 24. Brussels. Winter 2016.

· Edwards, E. Man and Machine: Systems for safety, in Proceedings of the BALPA Technical Symposium, London. 1972.

· Fuller, S. Kuhn vs. Popper: The Struggle for the Soul of Science. Allen & Unwin Pty. Ltd. Australia. 2006.

· Giddens, A., La constitution de la société. Éléments de la théorie de la structuration, Paris, PUF, 1987. (Cote : HM-24-G5314)

· Gill, G.W. Maritime Error Management. Discussing and Remediating Factors contributing to Casualties, Atglen, PA, Cornell Maritime Press, 2011.

· Hawkins, F.H., Human Factors in Flight, Aldershot, United Kingdom, Gower Technical Press, 1987.

· Kochan, T.A., Katz, H.C. and McKersie, R.B., (dir.) (1984). The Transformation of American Industrial Relations, 2nd edition. Ithaca. Cornell University Press.

· Hollnagel, E. et al. Resilience Engineering: Concepts and precepts. Taylor and Francis Group. CRC Press. 2006.

· Larouche, V., Déom, E., "L'approche systémique en relations industrielles," Relations industrielles, 1984, vol. 39, no 1.

· Lévesque, G-H, "Allocution du TRP," Rapport Annuel. 1945, p. 5.

· Loi sur les accidents du travail et les maladies professionnelles (LATMP) (LRRQ, chapitre A-3.001). 1985.

· Ministère de la Justice du Canada. Cours canadien de sécurité dans le maniement des armes à feu : Manuel de l'étudiant. Deuxième édition. ISBN 0-0660-95978-X. 1998.

· Mongeau, P. et Erpicum, D., "La pensée systémique. Historique et concepts," Revue L'orientation professionnelle, 1981, vol. 17, no 1.

· Morgan, G., "Reconnaître l'importance de l'environnement: des organisations vues comme des systèmes ouverts," images de l'organisation, Québec, Presses de l'Université Laval, 1989, pp. 39-44.

· Nagel, D.C., Human Error in Aviation Operations, in Weiner, E.L. et Nagel D.C., eds., Human factors in aviation, San Diego, California, Academic Press, 1988, pp. 263-303.

· Norman, D.A., Categorization of Action Slips, Psychological Review, 1981, 88 (1), pp. 1-15.

· Norman, D.A., The Psychology of Everyday Things, New York, Basic Books, 1988.

· Owen, C. et al., Risky Work Environments, Farnham, England, Ashgate. 2009.

· Rasmussen, J., The definition of human error and a taxonomy for technical system design. Rasmussen, J., Duncan, K. and Leplat, T J. New Technology and Human Error, Toronto, John Wiley & Sons, 1987.

· Reason, J. Achieving a Safety Culture: Theory and practice. Work and Stress, 1998, Vol.12. No. 3. pp. 293-306.

· Reason, J. Human error, New York, Cambridge University Press, 1990.

· Saint-Cerny, Anne-Marie, Une tragédie annoncée, Écosociété, Montréal, 2018, 344 pages.

· Wallerstein, I. Les sciences sociales battent de l'aile. Quel phénix renaîtra? Cahier de recherche sociologique, 1995, no 24.

· Woods, D. et al., Behind Human Error, Surrey, Ashgate Publishing Ltd., Second Edition, 2010.

· Wiegmann, D.A., Shappell, S.A. A human error approach to aviation accident analysis: The human factors analysis and classi-fication system. Burlington, VT: Ashgate Publishing, Ltd. 2003.

CHAPTER III

For an official account of the investigations on the airline disaster, you may wish to read the complete investigation reports. You can find links to PDF versions of the Spanish and Dutch reports here: https://en.wikipedia.org/wiki/Tenerife_airport_disaster. (Last accessed August 1, 2020)

I mention The World Values Survey (WVS). It is a global research project that explores people's values and beliefs, how they change over time, and their social and political impact. A worldwide network of social scientists in almost 100 countries supports this survey. Since 1981, they have conducted national surveys as part of WVS that measure, monitor, and analyze various factors: support for democracy; tolerance of foreigners and ethnic minorities; support for gender equality; the role of religion and changing levels of religiosity; the impact of globalization; attitudes toward the environment, work, family, politics, national identity, culture, diversity, insecurity; and subjective well-being.

The findings provide information for policymakers seeking to build civil society and democratic institutions. Governments, scholars, students, and journalists frequently use the results of the survey, as do international organizations and institutions such as the World Bank and the United Nations.

· Hofstede, G. Culture's Consequences: International Differences in Work-Related Values (2nd ed.). Beverly Hills CA: SAGE Publications. 1984.

· Hofstede, G. Dimensionalizing Cultures: The Hofstede Model in Context. ScholarWorks@GVSU. Online Readings in Psychology and Culture. 12-1-2011. Retrieved 03 February 2019.

· Hofstede, G. Cultures and Organizations: Software of the mind. London: McGraw-Hill. 1991.

· Hofstede, G, Culture's Consequences: Comparing values, behaviors, institutions, and organizations across nations. London, SAGE. 596 pages. 2001.

· ILO-OSH 2001 Guidelines on Occupational Safety and Health Management Systems, International Labour Organisation. 1 January 2009. ISBN 92-2-111634-4. http://www.admiraltylaw-guide.com/conven/ismcode1993.html.

· The International Safety Management Code, IMO Assembly Resolution A.741 (18) - 1993.

· Minkov, M. What Makes Us Different and Similar: A new interpretation of the World Values Survey and other cross-cultural data. Sofia, Bulgaria: Klasika y Stil Publishing House. 2007.

· Medvedev, G. The truth about Chernobyl (New York: Basic). 1991.

· Power, Nicole Gerarda. Constructing a 'Culture of Safety': An examination of the assumptions embedded in occupational safety and health curricula delivered to high school students and fish harvesters in Newfoundland and Labrador, Canada. Policy and Practice in Health and Safety. IOSH. 2010.

· Hollnagel, E., Leonhardt, J., Shorrock, S. and Licu, T. From Safety-I to Safety-II. A white paper. Brussels: EUROCONTROL Network Manager. 2013.

· Hollnagel, E. The Nitty-Gritty of Human Factors (Chapter 4). In S. Shorock and C. Williams (eds.), Human Factors and Ergonomics in Practice: Improving system performance and human well-being in the real world. Boca Raton, FL.: CRC Press. 2016.

· Orlady, H.W. and Orlady, L.M. Human Actors in Multi-crew Flight Operations. Ashgate. Brookfield, VT, USA. 1999.

· Reason, J. Achieving a Safety Culture: Theory and practice. Work and Stress, 1998. Vol.12. No. 3, pp. 293-306.

· Slocum, S. The Gatherer: Male bias in anthropology. Monthly Review Press. New York. 1975 also available at Slocum, Sally. Woman the gatherer: male bias in anthropology (1975), in McGee, R.J.; Warms, R.L. (eds.). Anthropological theory:

an introductory history. New York: McGraw-Hill. 2012. pp. 399-407.

CHAPTER IV

The investigation reports on the tanker *Nanny* can be found at www.tsb.gc.ca: M12H0012 and M14C0219.

You may want to see the TED talk by Marc Bonnant (in French) who provides more information on doubting: http://www.ekouter. net/de-la-defense-du-doute-avec-marc-bonnant-aux-conferences-ted-a-geneve-1657 (Last accessed August 1, 2020).

To read more about emotional and logical intelligence, I suggest Etienne Groleau's *L'oubli de la vie* (2018). You can also learn much on this topic from reading David Hume and Jean-Jacques Rousseau.

· Abbott, K. Industrial Relations Research: A Critical Realist Defence of its Theories and Methodologies, Actes du XLIe Congrès de l'ACRI, Concorde, Captus University Press, pp. 39-53. 2005.

· Audet, M., Larouche, V., "Paradigmes, écoles de pensée et théories en relations industrielles, Relations Industrielles." Philosophie des sciences sociales. vol. 43, no. 1, p. 11. 1988.

· Audet, M., Landry, M., Déry, R. "Sciences et résolution de problèmes : liens, difficultés et voies de dépassement dans le champ des sciences de l'administration." Philosophie des sciences sociales. vol. 16, pp. 409-410, 425-428, 433-435. 1986.

· Bradford, Alina. Deductive Reasoning vs. Inductive Reasoning. Live Science.com.

· Chalmers, A.F. Qu'est-ce que la science? Le livre de poche, Coll. Biblio-essais. Cote: Q-175-C4514. 1987.

· Déry, R. "L'impossible quête d'une science de la gestion," Gestion, Volume 20, numéro 3. Septembre 1995. p. 35.

· Flyvbjerg, B. Making Social Science Matter: Why social inquiry fails and how it can succeed again," Cambridge, Cambridge University Press, pp. 38-49, 129-140. 2001.

· Flyvbjerg, B. Megaprojects and Risk: An anatomy of ambition. Cambridge University Press. 2003.

· Fuller, Steve. "Kuhn vs. Popper: The struggle for the soul of science." Allen & Unwin Pty. Ltd. Australia. 2006.

· Goddar, J. "Theory and Method in Industrial Relations. Modernist and Postmodernist Alternatives," in R. Adams, N. Meltz, Industrial Relations Theory. Its Nature, Scope and Pedagogy, IMLR Press, Rutgers University, pp. 283-306. 1993.

· Groleau, E. "L'oubli de la vie, critique de la raison parodique." Éditions Liber. Montreal. 185 pages. 2018.

· Harari, Yuval Noah. Sapiens, A brief history of humankind. McClelland and Stewart. Penguin Random House. 2014. 450 pages.

· Heard E, Martienssen, R.A. Transgenerational Epigenetic Inheritance: Myths and mechanisms." Cell. 157 (1): pp. 95-109. 2014.

· Horgan, J. Profile: Paul Karl Feyerabend, the worst enemy of science. *Scientific American*. 268 (5): pp. 36-37. 1993.

· Huynh, Nancy, Cultural Cognition and Scientific Consensus, Yale Scientific Magazine, 2001.

· Kline, M. "Mathématiques. La fin des certitudes," Paris, C. Bourgeois. pp. 502-503. 1989.

· Kofman, Ava. Bruno Latour, the post-truth philosopher, mounts a defense of science. New York Times Magazine. October 25, 2018.

· Kuhn, T.S. The Structure of Scientific Revolutions: 50th anniversary. Ian Hacking (intro.) (4th ed.). University of Chicago Press. p. 264. 2012.

· Lenoir, S. "Une science pour les hommes de ce temps, " Le Monde diplomatique. Mars, 1990.

· Moore, D.S. The Developing Genome. Oxford University Press. 2015. ISBN 978-0-19-992234-5.

· Moysan-Lapointe, H. La vérité chez Protagoras. Laval théologique et philosophique. Érudit. 66 (3), pp. 529-545. 2010.

· Tapia, M., Ibsen, C.L., Kochan, T.A., Mapping the frontier of theory in industrial relations: the contested role of worker representation, Socio-Economic Review, Vol. 13, No. 1, pp. 157-184. Oxford University Press. 2015.

· Neidhart, W.J. "Possible Relationships Between Polanyi's Insights and Modern Findings in Psychology, Brain Research, and Theories of Science." JASA 31 (March 1979): pp. 61-62.

· Oehler, K. Protagoras from the Perspective of Modern Pragmatism. Transactions of the Charles S. Peirce Society, 38, 1-2. 2002, p. 210.

· Putnam, Robert D., and Sander, Thomas H. "Still Bowling Alone? The Post-9/11 Split." Journal of Democracy, Volume 21, Number 1, pp. 9-16. January 2010.

· Popper, Karl. Conjectures and Refutations. (1962). Harper, p. 123. 1968.

· Russell, Bertrand. The Principles of Mathematics. University Press, Cambridge, 1903. p. 5.

· Wallerstein, I. "Les sciences sociales battent de l'aile. Quel phénix renaîtra ? " Cahier de recherche sociologique, no. 24, pp. 209-213. 1995.

Research on Imre Lakatos is available in the *Stanford Encyclopedia of Philosophy* (on-line).

I recommend the following article by Nick Enfield if you are interested in learning more about pre-established beliefs: https://www.theguardian.com/commentisfree/2018/jul/20/

our-job-as-scientists-is-to-find-the-truth-but-we-must-also-be-storytellers. (Last accessed August 1, 2020)

Information on how we evolved and how we initially coexisted in groups of 50 up to 200 is well-documented and can be found in many publications and reports. I extracted some information from here: http://www.bbc.com/future/story/20120522-one-world-order (Last accessed August 1, 2020).

CHAPTER V

I used several publications to summarize the story of the *Deepwater Horizon*, including the Marine Casualty Investigation report: Office of the Maritime Administrator. Marshall Islands. 17 August 2011. Retrieved 4 December 2018. I also read Investigating the Cause of the Deepwater Horizon Blowout, *The New York Times*, 21 June 2010.

· Ariely, D. The honest truth about dishonesty, Harper Collins. p. 255. 2012.

· Associated Press. Laws of War: Opening of Hostilities (Hague III), October 18, 1907.

· DePaulo, Bella M. et al., Lying in Everyday Life, *Journal of Personality and Social Psychology*, 70, No. 5. May 1996. pp. 979, 984 and 987.

· Broder, John M.; Lewis, Neil A. (April 13, 1999). "Clinton is found to be in contempt on Jones lawsuit." *The New York Times*. p. 1.

· Butow, R.J. Marching Off to War on the Wrong Foot: the Final Note Tokyo Did not Send to Washington, 63. *Pacific Historical Review*, pp. 67-79. 1994.

· Cable, Timothy A. (judge) and Daniel M. "The Effect of Physical Height on Workplace Success and Income: Preliminary Test of a Theoretical Model." *Journal of Applied Psychology*, Vol. 89(3), Jun 2004, pp. 428-441.

· Costa, P.T. Jr. & McCrae, R.R. Revised NEO Personality Inventory (NEO-PI-R) and NEO Five-Factor Inventory (NEO-FFI) manual. Odessa, FL: Psychological Assessment Resources. 1992.

· Dunbar, Robin. Grooming, Gossip and the Evolution of language. Harvard University Press. Cambridge. 1998.

· Ekman, Paul and O'Sullivan, Maureen. "Who Can Catch a Liar?" *American Psychologist* 46, No. 9 (September 1991): pp. 913-20.

· Freitag, M. and Traunmüller, R. Spheres of trust: An empirical analysis of the foundation of particularized and generalized trust. *European Journal of Political Research*. 2009. pp. 782-803.

· Garber, Megan. "The Way We Lie Now," *The Atlantic*, September 2013, pp. 15-16.

· Goldberg, L. R. "The structure of phenotypic personality traits," American Psychologist. Vol. 48: pp. 26-34. 1993.

· Goleman, Daniel. Vital Lies, Simple Truths: the Psychology of Self Deception. Simon & Schuster, New York. 1996.

· Harari, Yuval Noah. Sapiens, A brief History of Humankind. McClelland and Stewart. Penguin Random House. 2014. 450 pages.

· Jackson, Robert L. (July 30, 1999). "Clinton Fined $90,686 for Lying in Paula Jones Case." *Los Angeles Times*. Gearan, Anne. October 1, 2001.

· Jung, C.G. Psychological Types. Princeton University Press. pp. 136-147. 1971.

· Kahan, Dan M. and Braman, Donald, "Cultural Cognition and Public Policy." Yale Law School Legal Faculty Series. 103. 2006.

· Kahan, Dan M. "Ideology, motivated reasoning, and cognitive reflection." Judgment and Decision Making, Vol. 8. No. 4, July 2013, pp. 407-424.

· Kraft, P.W., M. Lodge, and C.S. Taber. "Why people 'don't trust evidence': Motivated reasoning and scientific beliefs." *Annals of the American Academy of Political and Social Science* 685: 121-133. 2015.

· Lappé, Anthony and Marshall, Stephen. "True Lies," Guerrilla News Network, A Plume Book, Penguin Group, New York, 2004, p. xii.

· Lubin, Gus. *Business Insider*. BP CEO Tony Hayward apologizes for his idiotic statement: "I'd like my life back." June 2, 2010.

· McAllister, D. J. Affect- and Cognition-Based Trust as Foundations for Interpersonal Cooperation in Organizations. *Academy of Management Journal*, 38, 24-59. 1995.

· Meg, Kelly. *Washington Post*: President Trump has made 4,229 false or misleading claims in 558 days. https://www.washingtonpost.com/people/meg-kelly/

· Möllering, Guido. "The nature of trust: from Georg Simmel to a theory of expectation, interpretation and suspension." *Sociology*. Vol. 35, No 2 (May 2001) pp. 403-420.

· Mullins, Justin. Daily News, New Scientist, 8 September 2010.

· O'Hagan, Ellie May. Measles is on the rise. But telling anti-vaxxers they're stupid won't fix it. *The Guardian*. February 15, 2019.

· Pfeffer, Jeffrey. "Leadership BS," Stanford Graduate School of Business, HarperCollins Publishing, 2015, p. 38.

· Rawlings, B.L. Trust and PR Practice. Institute of Public Relations. December 2007. Last accessed on October 18, 2018: https://www.instituteforpr.org/wp-content/uploads/Rawlins-Trust-formatted-for-IPR-12-10.pdf (Last accessed August 1, 2020)

· Ricks, Thomas E. Churchill and Orwell: The Fight for Freedom. Penguin Books. New York. 2017, p. 267.

· Strout, Erin. "To Tell the Truth," *Sales and Marketing Management*, July 2002, p. 42.

· Taber, C.S., and M. Lodge. "Motivate skepticism in the evaluation of political beliefs." *American Journal of Political Science* 50(3): pp. 755-769. 2006.

· Walter, Kiechel. The Management Century. *Harvard Business Review*. November 2012.

The article by Keith Kahn-Harris (also adaptation from his book titled Denial: The Unspeakable Truth) titled "Denialism, what drives people to reject the truth" is a good read and contains the quote I took from Richard Sennett: https://www.theguardian.com/news/2018/aug/03/denialism-what-drives-people-to-reject-the-truth (Last accessed August 1, 2020)

I mention Professor Peter Sandman whom I met when I was an instructor at the Canadian Coast Guard College (1997-1999). He gave a session on risk communication during the On-Scene-Commander course I had developed and was teaching. To learn more on risk communication and on the genius of Professor Sandman, visit his website: https.//www.psandman.com. (Last accessed August 1, 2020)

For the material on cultural cognition, I used information and extracted a quote from the website culturalcognition.net. (Last accessed August 1, 2020)

I extracted the quote on risk communication from the World Health Organization website: https://www.who.int/risk-communication/background/en/. (Last accessed August 1, 2020)

I extracted the information about Edelman from their website: https://www.edelman.com/. It is a great read if you want to learn more about trust. The analysis of the data has resulted in profound findings, albeit with an interpretation that is their own. (Last accessed August 1, 2020)

I extracted the information about trust in government from Nik Nanos, chief data scientist, during a presentation he made as a member on a public panel and planning workshop put together by Positive Energy, a think tank led by Professor Monica Gattinger of the University of Ottawa. The title of the workshop was Canadian Energy Politics: growing polarization, growing frustration. The panel was held on October 22, 2018.

CONCLUSION

· American Airlines. AMR Corporation announces largest aircraft order in history with Boeing and Airbus. Press Release. July 20, 2011. http://news.aa.com/news/news-details/2011/AMR-Corporation-Announces-Largest-Aircraft-Order-In-History-With-Boeing-And-Airbus-07202011/default.aspx (Last accessed August 1, 2020)

· Boeing, G. "Visual Analysis of Nonlinear Dynamical Systems: Chaos, Fractals, Self-Similarity and the Limits of Prediction." Systems, 4(4), pp. 37-54. 2016.

· Boeing. "Boeing Launches 737 New Engine Family with Commitments for 496 Airplanes from Five Airlines." Press release. August 30, 2011.

· Clark, Nicola. "Jet Order by American Is a Coup for Boeing's Rival." *The New York Times*. July 20, 2011.

· Flight International. "Boeing firms up 737 replacement studies by appointing team." Flight Global. March 3, 2006. (Last accessed August 1, 2020)

· Flight International. "Airbus aims to thwart Boeing's narrowbody plans with upgraded 'A320 Enhanced'." Flight Global. 20 June 2006. (Last accessed August 1, 2020)

· Godt, Nick. "Crude oil to average $80 a barrel in 2010 - EIA." Market Watch. January 12, 2010. Retrieved April 1, 2019.

· Hill, Nathan. The Nix. London, Picador. Octavo. 2017. 625 pages.

· Kaplan, Thomas. "After Boeing Crashes, Sharp Questions About Industry Regulation Itself." *The New York Times*. March 26, 2019.

· Lazo, Luz; Schemm, Paul; Aratani, Lori. "Investigators find 2nd piece of key evidence on crash of Boeing 737 Max 8 in Ethiopia." *The Washington Post*. Retrieved April 4, 2019.

· Lorenz, Edward N. "Deterministic Nonperiodic Flow." Journal of the Atmospheric Sciences. 20 (2): pp. 130-141. March 1963.

· Monod, Jacques. Le hasard de la nécessité, Paris, Seuil, 1970, pp. 32-3, 37-52.

· O'Keeffe, Niall. "Caution welcomed: Boeing's 737 Max." Flight International. September 12, 2011.

· Ostrower, Jon. "What is the Boeing 737 Max Maneuvering Characteristics Augmentation System?" The Air Current. November 13, 2018. Retrieved April 3, 2019.

· Reals, Kerry. "Airbus outlines expected market impact of A320NEO." Flight International. 7 Dec 2010. Retrieved April 1, 2019.

· Reuters. "No public details on crashed Lion Air voice recorder until final report: Indonesian official." January 22, 2019. Retrieved April 3, 2019.

· Russell, Edward. "United goes airframer 'agnostic' on future orders." Flight Global. 4 October, 2017. Retrieved April 1, 2019.

· U.S. Department of Transportation. "Audit of Certification for the Boeing 737-Max 8 (2012-2017)." March 19, 2019. Retrieved April 3, 2019.

· Virgin America. "Virgin America places Airbus's 10,000th order: signs firm order for 60 new aircraft, including first order for eco-efficient A320neo" (Virgin America press release) https://web.archive.org/web/20151208013636/http://www. virginamerica.com/cms/about-our-airline/press/2011/Virgin-America-Confirms-Order-for-60-New-Aircraft.html (Last accessed August 1, 2020)

I speak about the number of deaths in the fishing industry. Please see IMO.org for the summary of deliberations of the September 25, 2018 sub-committee on implementation of IMO instruments for the reports on casualties to fishermen worldwide.

My thinking evolved after reading System under stress: energy decision-making in Canada and the need for informed reform. You can find the document here: https://www.uottawa.ca/ positive-energy/sites/www.uottawa.ca.positive-energy/files/system-under-stress.pdf. (Last accessed August 1, 2020)

IMAGE CREDITS

Figure 2 is taken from the work of Frank Hawkins in his book: F.H., Human Factors in Flight, Aldershot, United Kingdom, Gower Technical Press, 1987.

Figure 3 is inspired by James Reason in his book: Reason, J. *Human Error*, New York, Cambridge University Press, 1990.

Figure 4 comes from the grid reproduced in an article by Stephen Cobb that can be found here: https://www.welivesecurity. com/2017/12/18/adventures-cybersecurity-research/ (Last accessed August 1, 2020). He credits the grid to Douglas, Wildavsky, Flynn, Slovic, Kahan, etc.

Index

Acknowledgments

I have been privileged to work with many creative, insightful colleagues and employees whose intellectual stimulation lead to the creation of this book. I want to thank everyone who worked with me and under my supervision during my public service career. I am indebted to hundreds of academics and experts for the content of the five chapters. I am the unique party to blame if I poorly interpreted the science or improperly provided an account.

I wish to thank and acknowledge two brilliant individuals who went over a book that was in rough shape. Both the editor, Jim McRae, and Jacques Kéroack, the contributing editor, are savvy and highly skilled writers. I am grateful for their talent and expertise.

I am also obliged to two other people who have read the manuscript and provided insight and comments. First, I would like to thank and acknowledge Dr. Stephen Blank. He not only read the book, but he shared his views on the content and on my writing. I especially thank him for his wisdom and one candid comment he made: "You need to review the parts of your book that you enjoyed writing the most; those parts need work." He was right. After re-reading with his comment in mind, I realized I had to either edit or cut many parts of the book. Stephen Blank is one of the most accomplished academics I know. I am privileged that he accepted to write the Foreword.

Dr. Jon Stuart, a former colleague, an investigator and expert in human factors, agreed to read the manuscript and provided some valuable comments and references. He paid particular attention to the first chapters, his area of expertise.

Finally, and most importantly, I wish to thank professor Monica Gattinger, my partner in life. Many ideas in this book, and most importantly chapter five and the concluding thoughts, are the direct result of our ongoing discussions on her work as an academic and her various functions, including Director of the Institute for Science, Society and Policy at the University of Ottawa. She helped me along my struggle to better understand how humans fail and how we could tell the story of failure.